IMAGES
of America

AROUND
ANZA VALLEY

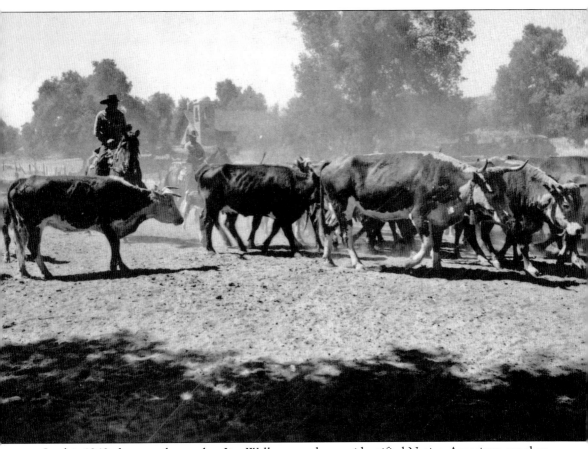

In this 1940 photograph, rancher Jim Wellman and an unidentified Native American rancher are moving cattle from the Santa Rosa Indian Reservation to what was then open range around Pinyon Flats. In the background the Santa Rosa Catholic Church can be seen. (Courtesy of the Hamilton Museum Collection.)

ON THE COVER: The branding of cattle is done to identify the animal's owner, which helps when cattle roam unfenced areas mixing with herds from other ranches. Branding day is hot and dirty work not only with the branding, but with other chores such as dehorning, castrating, and checking on the general health of the herd. For some, as in this picture, it was just a time of entertainment. (Courtesy of the Hamilton Museum Collection.)

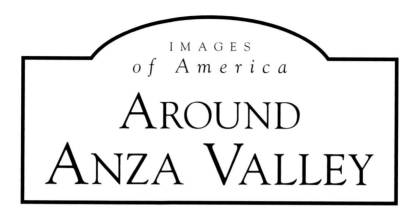

IMAGES
of America

AROUND
ANZA VALLEY

Margaret Wellman Jaenke, Tony Mauricio,
and the Hamilton Museum

ARCADIA
PUBLISHING

Published by Arcadia Publishing
Charleston SC, Chicago IL, Portsmouth NH, San Francisco CA

Printed in the United States of America

Library of Congress Catalog Card Number: 2007933020

For all general information contact Arcadia Publishing at:
Telephone 843-853-2070
Fax 843-853-0044
E-mail sales@arcadiapublishing.com
For customer service and orders:
Toll-Free 1-888-313-2665

Visit us on the Internet at www.arcadiapublishing.com

This book is dedicated to the countless people mentioned in Around
Anza Valley *whose many contributions made the region what it was and
what it is today.*

CONTENTS

ACKNOWLEDGMENTS

Thanks to Jayne Richardson, Jackie Spanley, and Brenda Fries for proofreading.

Special thanks also go to Jayne Richardson for keeping the Hamilton Museum operating as this book was being written.

Thanks go to pioneer descendants Margaret Teague, Gini Spencer, Raini Cunningham, and Ruth Roman for hours spent checking historical and cultural accuracy, as well as for proofreading.

Our many thanks go to the following who contributed their photograph collections in support of this book.

Anza Electric Co-Op Inc.
Ray Barmore
Bahrman photographs (Courtesy of Edell Lashley.)
William and Barbara Bradford photographs (Courtesy of Barbara Bradford.)
Violet Cary photographs (Courtesy of Dick Cary.)
Harriet Bergman Costo
Fanny Contreras photographs (Courtesy of the Hamilton Museum Collection.)
Clarena Dennis
W. L. Faust photographs (Courtesy of Shirley Harbeck.)
Vermal "Bud" Clark photographs (Courtesy of Mary Clark Garbani.)
Garner Valley Volunteer Firemen
Ione Hall photographs (Courtesy of Roger and Alice Hall.)
Louise Hamilton photographs (Courtesy of the Hamilton Museum Collection.)
Alice Hopkins
Verna Parks McFarlin
Mary E. Parks
Harry Quinn
Robert Tyler
Phil Valdez Jr.
Bud and Bobbie Wellman
James F. Wellman Sr. photographs (Courtesy of the Hamilton Museum Collection.)

INTRODUCTION

The Cahuilla people were the first inhabitants in the hilly region in and around Anza Valley in south central Riverside County, California. For thousands of years, these people hunted and gathered at an elevation between 3,000 and 6,000 feet.

In the 1770s, Juan Bautista de Anza traveled through the region on his expeditions to San Francisco giving the natives their first contact with other people. Hunters, trappers, and miners penetrated the hills on a temporary basis in the early 1800s. In the 1860s, cattlemen began to settle on a permanent basis.

Some of the early families who settled on homestead land around Cahuilla Mountain were the Parks, Reeds, and Tripps. The James Hamilton family settled in Cahuilla, later known as Anza. The Jacob Terwilliger family and the Clark brothers, Fred and Frank, settled to the south. The Thomas, Wellman, and Arnaiz families settled east of Anza in Hemet Valley, which is now called Garner Valley. All these families came to the area to take advantage of the excellent grazing land for their cattle. In winter, they moved their livestock into the lower elevations in Coyote Canyon and the Pinyon Flats area. Cattle from all the ranches roamed together over the unfenced hills and valleys. Roundups required the cooperation of all the ranchers helping one another not only with the actual gathering of the cattle throughout the entire area, but also with the sorting, branding, earmarking, and castrating. The cattle ready for market then had to be driven to the rail-shipping yard at San Jacinto, Temecula, or even San Bernardino.

Close friendships developed not only among the ranch families but also between the ranchers and the native people and their families. Native American cowboys working with the ranchers were among the best and usually took part in the roundups and brandings, sometimes as hired help, but often as friends.

In 1909, more land became available for homesteads bringing an increase in the population. Rather than becoming cattle ranchers, many of these new homesteaders were dry farmers raising oats, wheat, and other grain crops without irrigation. Dry farming continued to be a main occupation until the first deep irrigation well was dug in 1949. That well completely changed the area farming. With water available, the growing of irrigated commercial crops like potatoes and alfalfa was possible.

Up until the 1950s, life in and around Anza was much like life in the 1800s in other parts of the country. There were only dirt roads and no modern conveniences. The only churches were the Catholic churches at the Cahuilla and Santa Rosa Indian Reservations. Mail came once or twice a week. The one or two stores carried only basic goods. One-room schools or a home with one teacher educated the children of the ranchers and the homestead people.

In the mid-1950s, improvements like paved roads, telephones, and electricity brought the entire region into the 20th century. Soon doctors, dentists, better schools, a hardware store, a bank, a more complete grocery store, and other conveniences were all saving the residents a 30-mile trip down the hill for their basic needs.

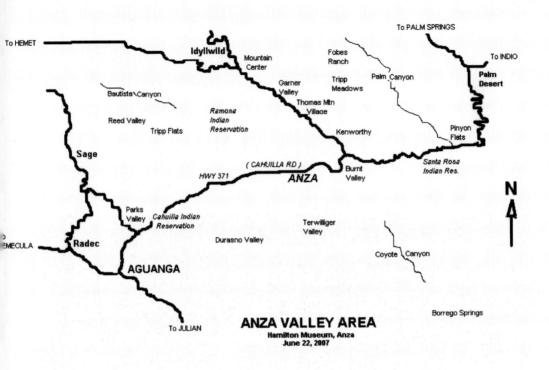

To HEMET

Idyllwild

To PALM SPRINGS

To INDIO

Mountain
Center

Fobes
Ranch

Palm
Desert

Garner
Valley

Tripp
Meadows

Palm Canyon

Bautista Canyon

Thomas Mtn
Village

Ramona
Indian
Reservation

Reed Valley

Tripp Flats

Kenworthy

Pinyon
Flats

Sage

(CAHUILLA RD)

Santa Rosa
Indian Res.

HWY 371

ANZA

Burnt
Valley

N

Parks
Valley

Cahuilla Indian
Reservation

Terwilliger
Valley

EMECULA

Radec

Durasno Valley

Coyote   Canyon

AGUANGA

ANZA VALLEY AREA

Borrego Springs

To JULIAN

Hamilton Museum, Anza
June 22, 2007

This is the map of the Anza Valley area covered in this publication with references to major locations such as Idyllwild, Palm Desert, Hemet, and Temecula. Other sites on the map retain their old names, so the reader may get a better feel for the area as these sites are mentioned in the following narrative. The map was drawn by Tony Mauricio.

One

FIRST RESIDENTS

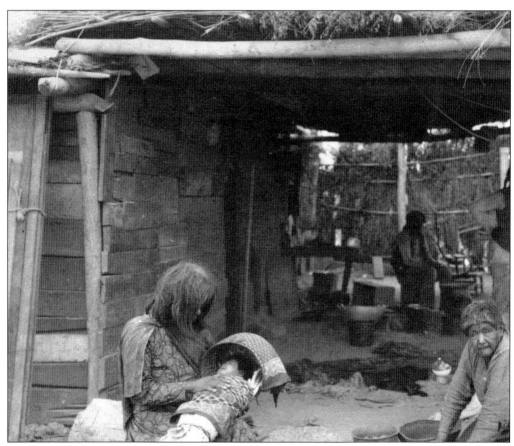

As detailed in many books on Cahuilla life, the Cahuilla Indians have lived in and around Anza Valley for thousands of years, surviving by hunting and gathering. This 1800s photograph illustrates how the Cahuilla continued to live in this isolated region much as they had before the first outsiders arrived. Current signs of ancient Cahuilla life throughout the mountains are the numerous bedrock mortars, used for grinding food. (Courtesy of Barbara Bradford.)

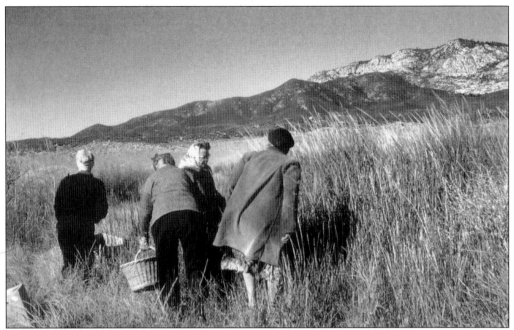

In 1955, these Native American women were collecting basket-making material on the Cahuilla Indian Reservation. Many kinds of native grasses and reeds found in the area are used in the lengthy process. In recent years, the Cahuilla people have kindled more interest in basketry among their young people so that the art of basket-making is not lost. (Courtesy of the Hamilton Museum Collection.)

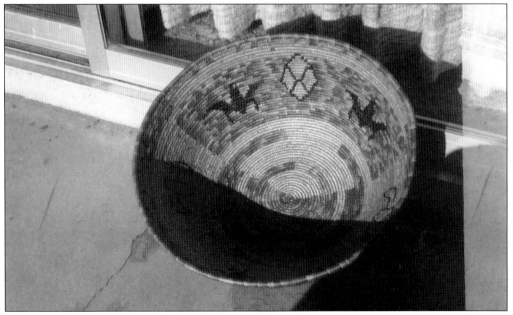

The Cahuilla baskets are widely known for their beauty, excellent workmanship, and for their artistry. Only natural materials and dyes are used to make the elaborate baskets. The basket designs often include images of rattlesnakes, lightning, and flowers. (Courtesy of the Hamilton Museum Collection.)

The life of Ramona Lubo, a mountain Cahuilla woman, was the inspiration for the fictional book *Ramona*, by Helen Hunt Jackson, as well as the play entitled *The Ramona Pageant*. Ramona, a lifelong mountain resident, lived to the west of Anza at Juan Diego Flat, which was named for her husband. (Courtesy of the Hamilton Museum Collection.)

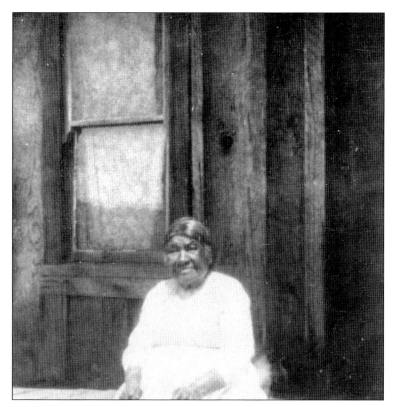

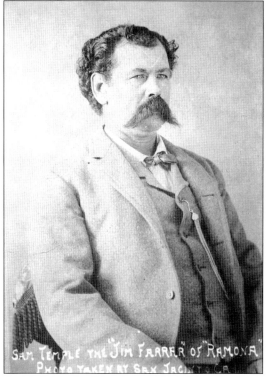

Sam Temple, the murderer of Ramona Lubo's husband, Juan Diego, was named Jim Farrar in both the book by Jackson and *The Ramona Pageant*. The pageant, performed in Hemet annually since 1923, is reputedly the longest-running outdoor play in California. Temple also had a colorful reputation as a teamster who hauled lumber down the mountain from Idyllwild to San Jacinto at full speed. (Courtesy of Mary Clark Garbani.)

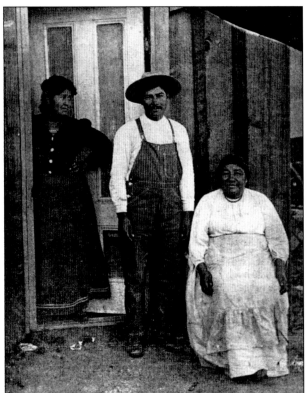

After Juan Diego was murdered, Ramona Lubo lived the rest of her life on the Cahuilla Indian Reservation in Anza near where Sam Temple shot her husband. Here she poses with her son Condino Diego and his wife. Ramona was buried at the Cahuilla Cemetery, a place that, over the years, has attracted tourists wishing to view her grave site. (Courtesy of the Hamilton Museum Collection.)

This is the site of Ramona's grave in the burial ground at Cahuilla Indian Reservation as it was in the early 1920s. In addition to being a tourist attraction, Ramona's grave site has been visited by performers of *The Ramona Pageant* who posed there for photographs. It was the location of at least one wedding performed in the 1930s by the local justice of the peace. (Courtesy of the Hamilton Museum Collection.)

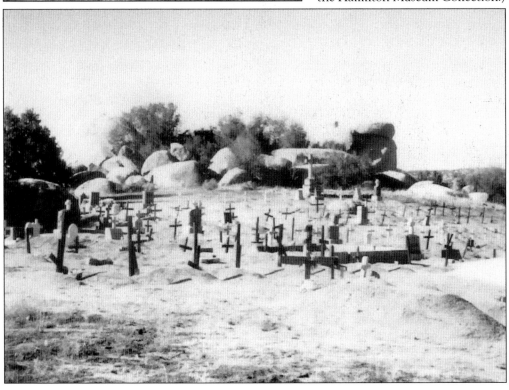

Two

NEWCOMERS

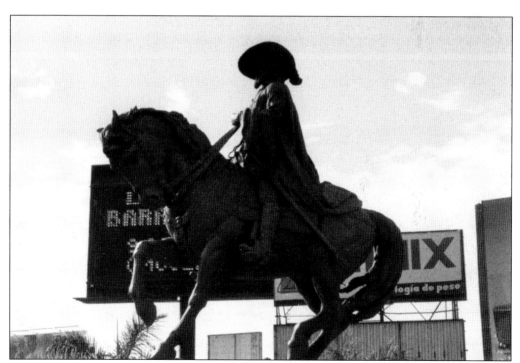

One of the first, besides the native people, to arrive in the hill country around Anza was a Spaniard, Juan Bautista de Anza. Anza first came through what became Anza in 1774 to explore a route over which to move settlers to San Francisco the following year. This statue of Juan Bautista de Anza is in Hermosillo, Sonora, Mexico, where the expedition began September 29, 1775. (Courtesy of Phil Valdez Jr.)

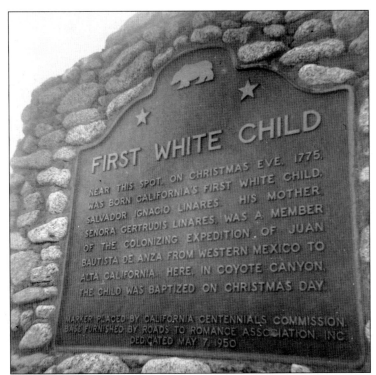

FIRST WHITE CHILD

NEAR THIS SPOT, ON CHRISTMAS EVE, 1775, WAS BORN CALIFORNIA'S FIRST WHITE CHILD. SALVADOR IGNACIO LINARES. HIS MOTHER SENORA GERTRUDIS LINARES, WAS A MEMBER OF THE COLONIZING EXPEDITION OF JUAN BAUTISTA DE ANZA FROM WESTERN MEXICO TO ALTA CALIFORNIA. HERE, IN COYOTE CANYON, THE CHILD WAS BAPTIZED ON CHRISTMAS DAY.

MARKER PLACED BY CALIFORNIA CENTENNIALS COMMISSION. BASE FURNISHED BY ROADS TO ROMANCE ASSOCIATION, INC. DEDICATED MAY 7, 1950

This monument south of Anza in Coyote Canyon commemorates the birth of one of the babies born during the second Juan Bautista de Anza expedition. Folklore has it that the child, Salvador Linares, was the first white child born in California, but research has revealed that his father was a full-blooded Native American and his mother, Gertrudis Rivus, was of mixed Spanish and Native American blood. (Courtesy of Phil Valdez Jr.)

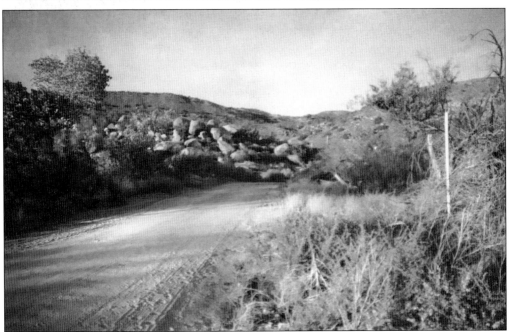

A Catholic priest, Padre Font, accompanying the 1775 Anza expedition, was very precise in recording landmarks that might be of importance. With modern technology, it has been found that he very accurately recorded the number of leagues traveled each day. This rock formation in Coyote Canyon, which Padre Font mentions in his diary, has been located using his descriptions along with modern locating systems. (Courtesy of Phil Valdez Jr.)

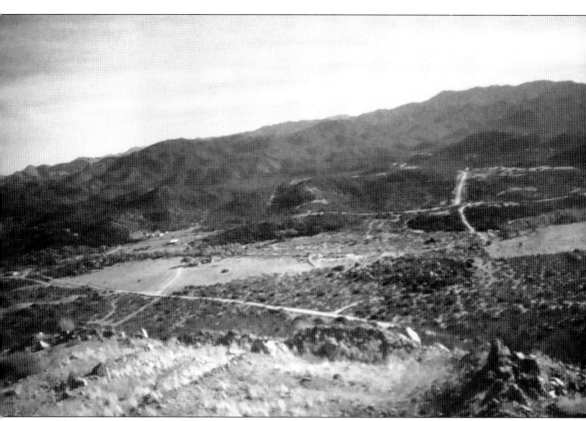

With information garnered from the diaries of Juan Bautista de Anza and Padre Font, as well as with the use of modern technology, this photograph taken in 2006 is identified as the location of the December 1774 expedition's Camp 55. The area is a part of the old Fred Clark Ranch, known since the 1930s as the Cary Ranch, where Art and Violet Cary and sons Bob and Dick ranched for many years. In 1924, a plaque describing both the 1774 and 1775 expeditions was placed on the Clark property. (Courtesy of Phil Valdez Jr.)

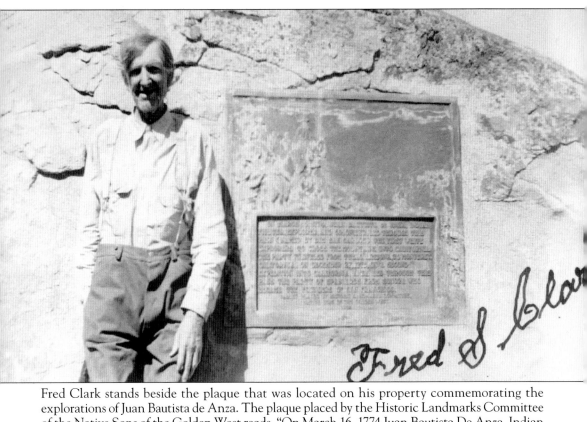

Fred Clark stands beside the plaque that was located on his property commemorating the explorations of Juan Bautista de Anza. The plaque placed by the Historic Landmarks Committee of the Native Sons of the Golden West reads, "On March 16, 1774 Juan Bautista De Anza, Indian fighter, explorer, and colonizer, led through this pass (named by him San Carlos) the first white explorers to cross the mountains into California. On December 27, 1775, on a second expedition, into California, Anza led through this pass the party of Spaniards from Sonora who became the founders of San Francisco." According to an article in an old Hemet newspaper, politicians, dignitaries, and other interested persons attended the ceremony on May 25, 1924. Two of the locals mentioned as attending were Mrs. Ike (Inez) Parks and Mrs. Joe (Clara) Hamilton. (Courtesy Dick Cary.)

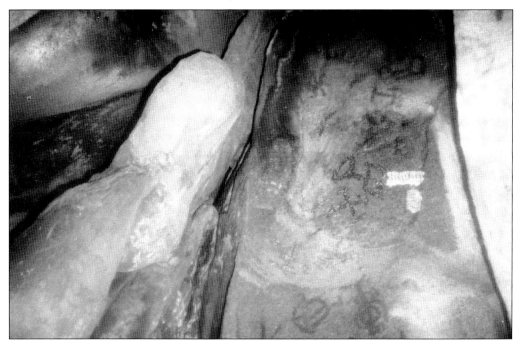

It is thought that Juan Bautista de Anza was the first person of European descent to have any contact with the Cahuilla people. These petroglyphs, or picture writings, at the Cary Ranch are believed to depict the passing of Juan Bautista de Anza through the valley. (Courtesy of Phil Valdez Jr.)

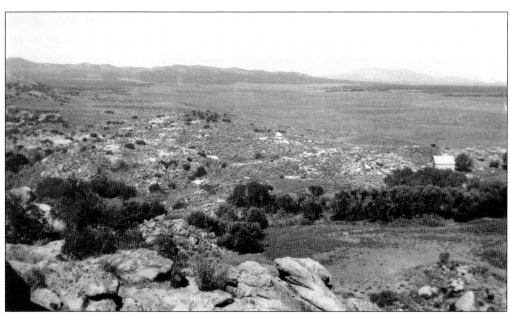

This photograph is of the view Anza and his party would have seen as they left their camp south of Anza, making their way toward present-day Bautista Canyon and the lower country. Bautista Canyon is in the gap just to the right of Cahuilla Mountain in the right background. It was still many days until the party reached their destination in San Francisco. (Courtesy Dick Cary.)

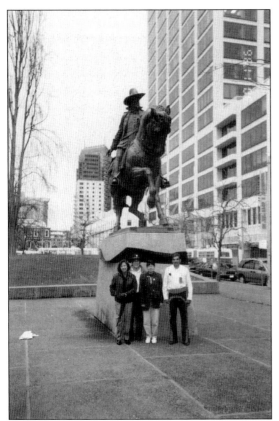

This statue (left), at what became known as San Francisco, commemorates the end of the long and dangerous journey of Juan Bautista de Anza and his fellow travelers. After weeks of trekking through hot deserts and snow-covered mountains while enduring thirst, hunger, births, and deaths, they arrived with their livestock and their household goods. Everything had been hauled all the way from Mexico on mules or horses. The Presidio de San Francisco and what was to become the city of San Francisco was founded. Descendants of some of those intrepid settlers often visit the memorial and take part in reenactments of the 1770s expeditions. Pictured (below) are five descendants of the Juan Bautista de Anza Expedition of 1775. Descendants are, from left to right, Katherine Johnson, Phil Valdez Jr., unidentified, Paul Bernal, and Janice Zinniker. (Courtesy of Phil Valdez Jr.)

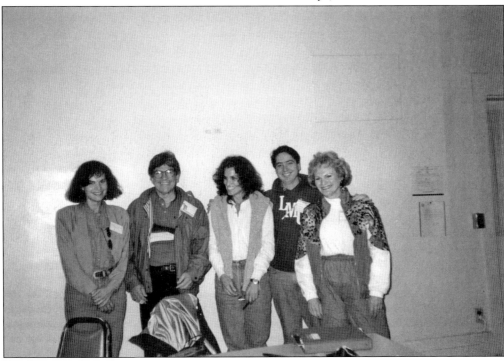

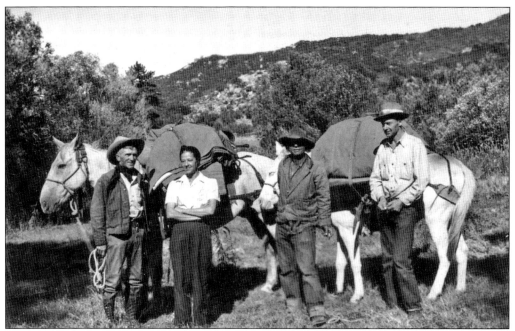

For many years, the Cahuilla people hunted animals for food. By the early 1800s, others ventured into the mountains to hunt and act as hunting guides when other work was scarce. In 1945, this group of hunters with food and equipment loaded on horses is ready to be led into the wilderness above Palm Canyon by guide Ernest Arnaiz, second from the right. (Courtesy of Bud and Bobbie Wellman.)

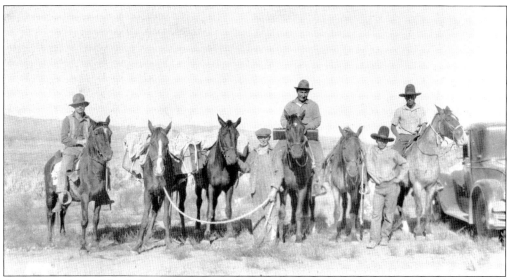

Several members of the Bahrman family are all packed up and ready to leave on a deer-hunting trip starting from their homestead in the Terwilliger area. From left to right in this 1930s photograph are an unidentified hunter; Carl Bahrman holding a rope; Bahrman's son-in-law Ed Durrent, holding a portable camp stove; and Carl's sons Milton, standing, and Lincoln, mounted. (Courtesy of Edell Lashley.)

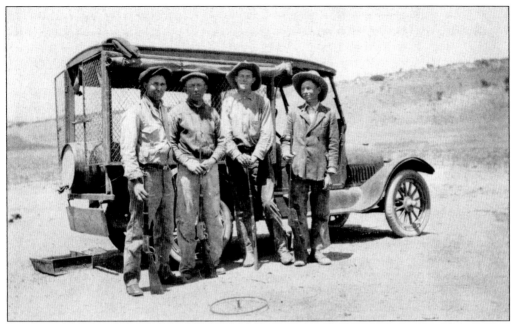

Well into the 1940s, many residents hunted rabbits and deer for food. Sometimes rabbits were so plentiful and so destructive in the grain fields that rabbit drives were organized to rid the fields of the pests. These four hunters, including Bud Clark (second from right) pose with their rifles before they set off on a deer hunt. (Courtesy of Mary Clark Garbani.)

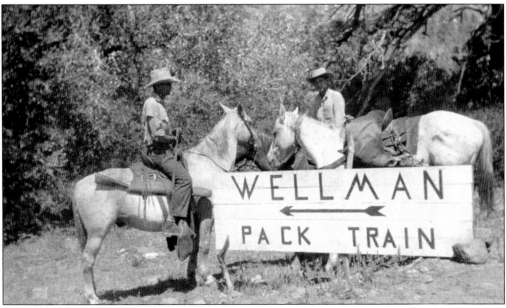

Sometimes hunting camps were established as a seasonal business, with hunters from the city returning year after year to their favorite hunting camp to be packed into the wilderness. In 1937, Jim Wellman and his 16-year-old son, Bud Wellman, return to one such camp at Tripp Meadows with a deer that was bagged on the desert side of the mountain above Palm Canyon. (Courtesy of Bud and Bobbie Wellman.)

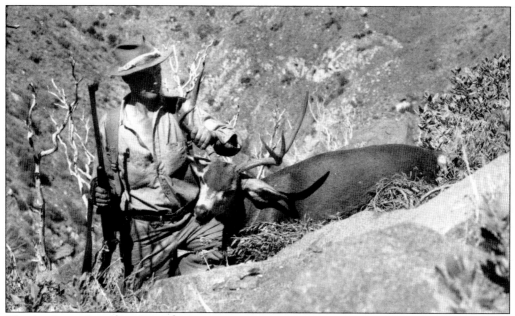

This buck was bagged in West Fork Canyon above Palm Springs. The canyon was an excellent hunting area and also one where the cattle ranchers wintered their livestock. Sometimes the cattle roamed even farther down the rocky slopes onto the desert floor. The ranchers also hunted mountain lions, because lions destroyed their cattle. Hunting was the only means to keep the predators under control. (Courtesy of Bud and Bobbie Wellman.)

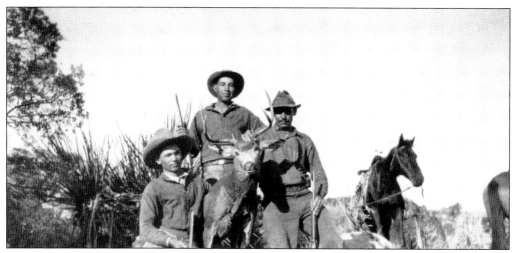

In approximately 1920, Jim Wellman, Lincoln Hamilton, and an unidentified hunter rest with a good-sized deer after a successful hunt. To save the meat, jerky was made by cutting the venison into strips and hanging it on a line to air dry. The dried meat would keep indefinitely without refrigeration, a plus where there was no electricity. (Courtesy of the Hamilton Museum Collection.)

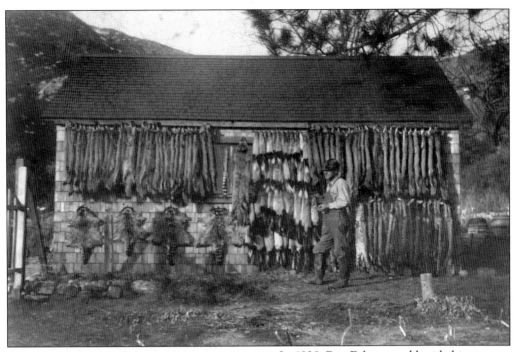

In 1928, Ray Fobes stood beside his catch of animal furs at his home in Fobes Canyon. Note the drying pelts of many different kinds of animals. Children of the day also found trapping to be a good means of making a little money. Some children even had a trap line they could tend on their way to and from school, catching everything from foxes to gophers. (Courtesy of the Hamilton Museum Collection.)

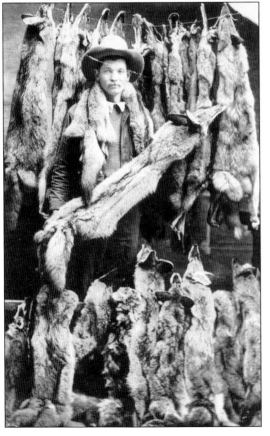

One industrious child attempting to earn some cash caught a skunk on his way to school. He took the live skunk to school with the intent to scare the girls. The intended prank literally backfired when the student got sprayed by the skunk. Known as a prankster in his own right but who was serious about trapping was Jim Wellman, shown with some of his pelts. (Courtesy of the Hamilton Museum Collection.)

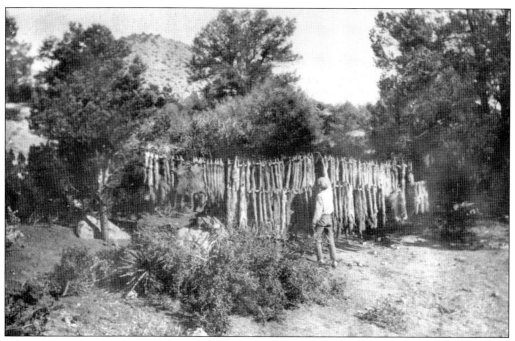

Trapping was usually done during the winter when the animal furs were at their thickest and best. In 1928, Ray Fobes and the Jim Wellman family took this catch on Pinyon Flats near Sugar Loaf Mountain. The furs were placed on stretchers to dry. After drying, the pelts were sent by mail to a tannery. (Courtesy of the Hamilton Museum Collection.)

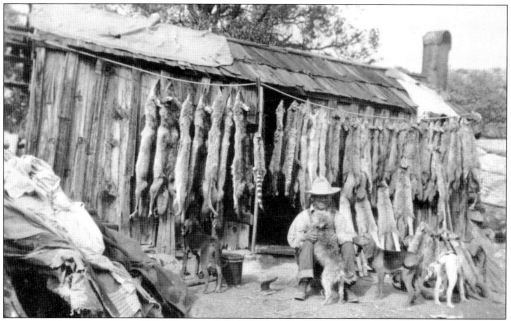

Since the 1800s, a cattle camp existed at Asbestos Springs in the Pinyon Flats area. It was also used by hunters, trappers, and prospectors as a base camp. Coyotes, foxes, ring-tailed cats, skunks, and other animals were all fair game, giving trappers a means to earn money at times when employment was difficult to find. (Courtesy of the Hamilton Museum Collection.)

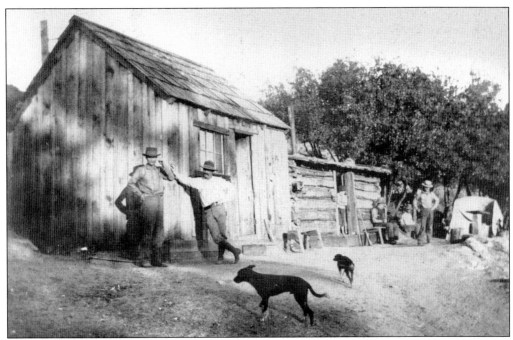

In the late 1800s, Eames Chilson, pictured in the white shirt, owned this miner's cabin and the Hemet Belle Mine in Kenworthy. Chilson liked to impress upon people, including wealthy Englishman Harold Kenworthy, that he was a successful miner by reputedly lighting his cigars with $10 bills. Kenworthy, though, had no knowledge of the "salting" (secretly placing gold to make it seem as if a mine is producing) Chilson is rumored to have done. When Chilson, to prove the mine had gold, shot into the rocks of the mine, little did Kenworthy know that Chilson was actually shooting buckshot laced with gold dust. As a result, Kenworthy paid Chilson the outrageous sum of $120,000 for the mine. (Courtesy of the Hamilton Museum Collection.)

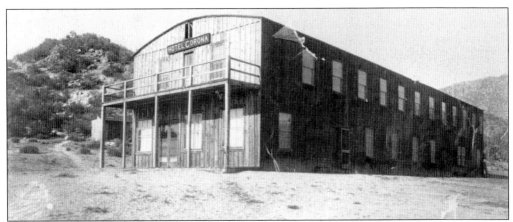

Harold Kenworthy immediately began construction of homes, a school, a hotel, and commercial buildings in what became a town of over 200 people. The two-story Hotel Corona was said to have had running water and be able to comfortably accommodate at least 60 guests at one time. Water for the town was piped from nearby Pipe Creek Canyon. (Courtesy of the Hamilton Museum Collection.)

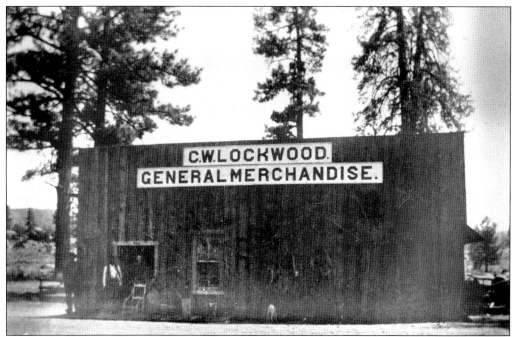

C. W. Lockwood General Merchandise, a store that furnished the townspeople and nearby ranchers with their basic needs, also housed the Kenworthy Post Office. The life of the town of Kenworthy was short-lived with the Kenworthy School, which was built by Harold Kenworthy, outliving the entire town, including the C. W. Lockwood General Merchandise. (Courtesy of the Hamilton Museum Collection.)

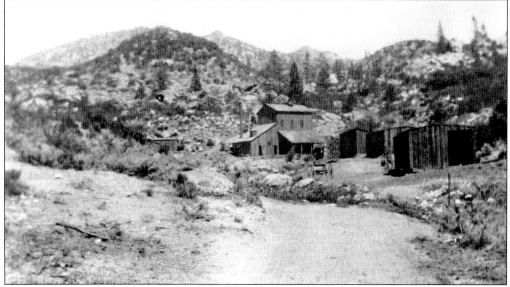

Harold Kenworthy entered into the mining business with high hopes, which were never realized. Such little gold was found that the assay office and the stamp mill were never put to real use. Realizing the mine would never be as productive as he had believed, Kenworthy gave up after a couple years, selling his share for only $10 before leaving the country. (Courtesy of the Hamilton Museum Collection.)

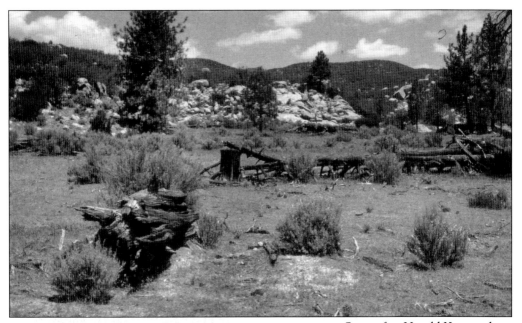

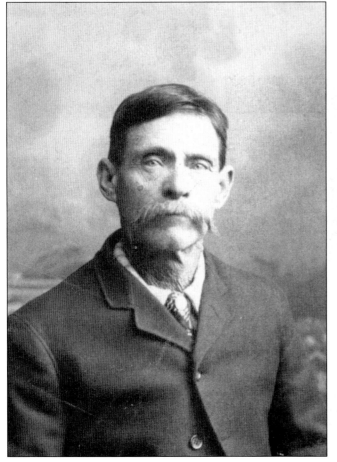

Soon after Harold Kenworthy departed from Kenworthy, all the equipment and lumber from the town's buildings was removed from the area. It was reused in other parts of the hills. The town was abandoned, but it never had a chance to become a real ghost town. Today there is no sign of the mining town of Kenworthy. (Courtesy of the Hamilton Museum Collection.)

Jesus Contreras was a luckier miner than Harold Kenworthy. While prospecting in the hills east of Garner Valley during the 1860s, Contreras found so much gold that he buried a part of it. With the remainder, he returned to his home in Colton with the intent of recovering the buried gold later when he might need it. (Courtesy of the Hamilton Museum Collection.)

When Jesus Contreras finally did return to the hill country many years later in the early 1900s to recover his stashed gold, he brought with him his two grandsons, Antone and John Contreras. The buried gold was never located, but the younger men did find brides at the nearby Mañuel and Dolores Arnaiz homestead. After brief courtships, Antone Contreras married Daisy Arnaiz (right) and his brother John married Fanny Arnaiz, Daisy's younger sister (below). These two couples were the first to file on homestead land in Anza after the land became available in 1909. Fanny and John's homestead property on South Contreras Road is the present home of the Hamilton Museum. (Courtesy of the Hamilton Museum Collection.)

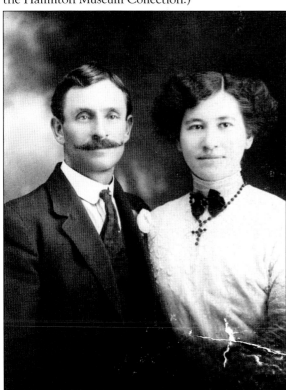

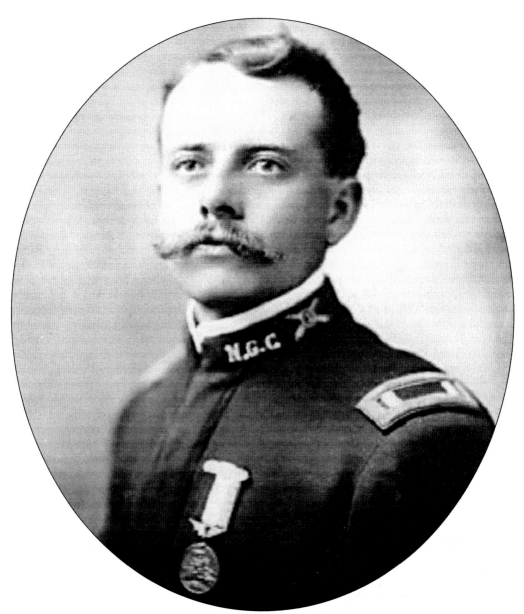

Prospectors and miners searched throughout the hills for other minerals besides gold. Cahuilla Mountain had its share of quartz mines. The New Columbia tourmaline mine on Thomas Mountain was a thriving operation in the 1800s and early 1900s. The Garnet Queen Mine on the slopes of Santa Rosa Mountain had its day. Asbestos mining at Pinyon Flats was a lucrative business over the years for many different operators. This picture is of Elmer E. Dunn, age 27, wearing his National Guard of Colorado Uniform. He was a sergeant with the Battery A Field Artillery. The picture was taken about 1898 at the time of the Spanish-American War. Prospecting and mining were in Dunn's blood, having grown up in the mines west of Denver. Dunn actively prospected and mined in the Pinyon Flats area from the 1930s through the 1950s. He held numerous claims and operated an asbestos mine in the area. Even today, people find his rock corner claim markers with the old tobacco can still in place. (Courtesy of Harry Quinn.)

Three

CATTLEMEN

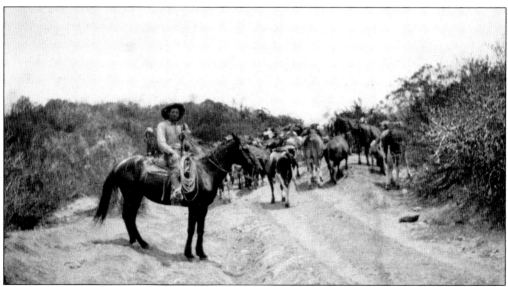

Raising cattle was hard work, requiring many hours in the saddle often in the hot sun or freezing weather. These cattle are being moved in 1920 from Anza Valley up over the Hamilton Grade for summer grazing in the cooler higher elevations of Kenworthy and Tripp Meadows. For winter grazing, the cattle were usually moved to warmer Coyote and Palm Canyons, depending on the availability of feed. (Courtesy of the Hamilton Museum Collection.)

UNITED STATES DEPARTMENT OF AGRICULTURE
FOREST SERVICE
CLEVELAND NATIONAL FOREST

SAN DIEGO, CALIFORNIA.
July 31, 1909.

G
Cleveland,Permits,C & H.
Arnaiz, Manuel, #86

Mr. Manuel Arnaiz,
Through Deputy Ranger Spence,
Hemet, Calif.

Dear Sir:

You will recall our conversation about the wild
cattle east of the Hemet Valley:

Please make a determined effort to rid the range
of these cattle, at least by September 30.

I believe Messrs. Hamilton Bros., Garner and Tripp
will gladly cooperate in the work, they have been
written to.

Very truly yours,

Forest Supervisor.

E

Keeping the cattle where they were supposed to be was sometimes a problem. Cattle often strayed off while on open range or became lost during cattle drives. Over the years, they became wild. This July 31, 1909, letter from the U.S. Forest Service to Manuel Arnaiz requests that he get assistance from cattlemen Hamilton, Garner, and Tripp to remove the wild cattle from national forestland. (Courtesy of the Hamilton Museum Collection.)

This receipt, dated September 20, 1901, and signed by Manuel Arnaiz, is for the work Arnaiz did rounding up and driving cattle from the mountain area to San Bernardino. Arnaiz earned the $19.80 for the four days of work, a good sum at the time. The cattle were driven to San Bernardino to be sold in order to settle the estate of his recently deceased son-in-law, Frank Wellman. (Courtesy of the Hamilton Museum Collection.)

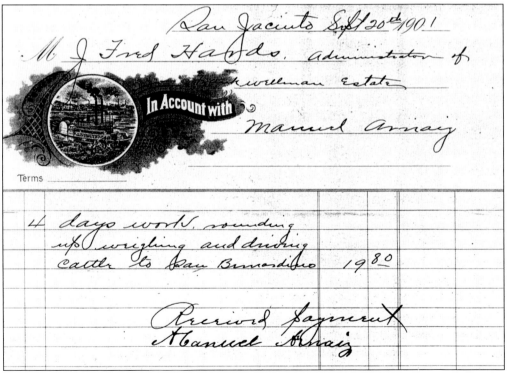

On the open (unfenced) range, cattle often strayed onto other people's property. In this September 6, 1910, letter, the U.S. Indian Service ordered Manuel Arnaiz to immediately remove his cattle from the Native American reservation or face a $1-per-head fine. (Courtesy of the Hamilton Museum Collection.)

DEPARTMENT OF THE INTERIOR

UNITED STATES INDIAN SERVICE

Cahuilla School,

Cahuilla, Calif., Sept. 6, 1910.

Mr. Manuel Arnaiz,

　　at Home,

Dear Sir;-

　　　　The Indians report that there are a number of head of your cattle on the reservation.　I have issued wire to them to construct a drift fence across Palm Canon　and they are ready to begin the fence.　You should drive your cattle out of there at once and keep them out, as I have instructed the Indian Police to corral all cattle trespassing on that reservation, and notify me of his action, when I shall be obliged to make a charge of $1. per head as provided by law for all such cattle corralled. The other cattle men have removed their cattle and paid the damages assessed promptly, and I will expect the same in your case.

　　　　　　　　Very respectfully,

　　　　　　　　Francis A. Swayne

　　　　　　　　Superintendent.

These four mounted riders, including two young boys, are ready for a day of riding. As soon as ranch children were able to sit on a horse, they helped out with the cattle. By the time they were 10 or 12 years old, they were usually quite experienced in handling cattle. (Courtesy of the Hamilton Museum Collection.)

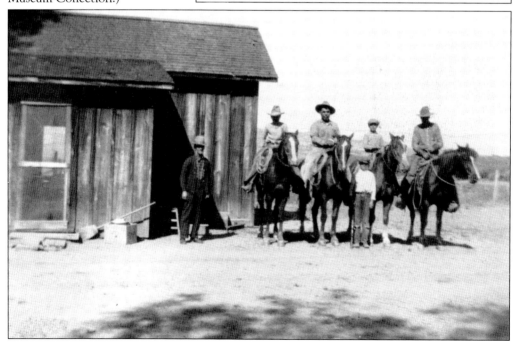

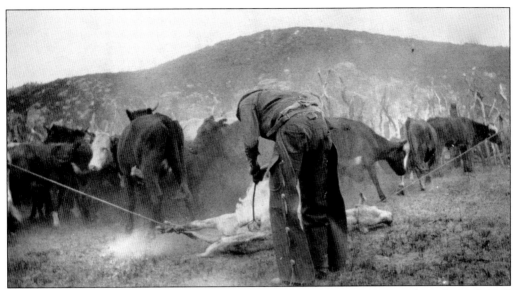

In the 1920s, Lincoln Hamilton was still using his grandfather's, James Hamilton, "open heart" branding iron to brand his own cattle. Note the pole corral that was made from brush cleared from the fields. (Courtesy of Bud and Bobbie Wellman.)

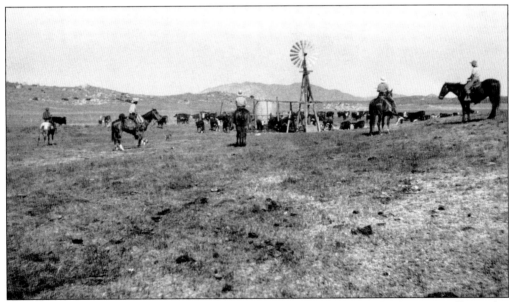

Pictured here in 1937 photograph are, from left to right, an unidentified rider, Jim Wellman, his wife Elma, and their daughters Margaret and Clarena getting ready to round up Wellman cattle on the Cahuilla Indian Reservation. Many cattle ranchers leased the greener pastures on the reservation where water was more plentiful. Cahuilla Mountain can be seen in the background. (Courtesy of Bud and Bobbie Wellman.)

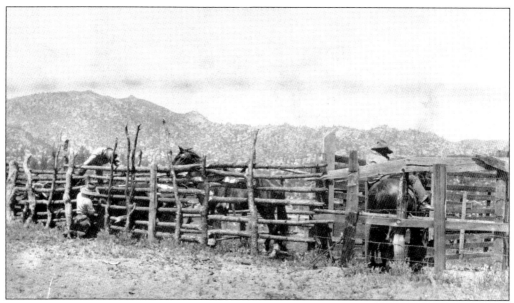

Prior to the Hamilton, Wellman, and Arnaiz families building this branding chute in Kenworthy around 1926, the branding of cattle took place in either a corral or open pasture. Confining the animal to be branded in the branding chute made it faster and easier to get the job done with the larger cattle. The calves and smaller cattle continued to be roped for branding. (Courtesy of Bud and Bobbie Wellman.)

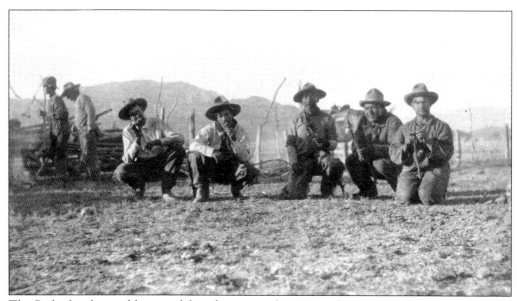

The Parks family, neighbors, and friends are rounding up cattle in 1912 to be sold to settle the estate of Frances Parks, widow of David Parks. The participants are, from left to right, Lincoln Parks (son of Frances Parks), Quitman Reed, Spencer White, Pete Hibbert, unidentified, Domingo Costo, and Sal Biles. (Courtesy of Mary E. Parks.)

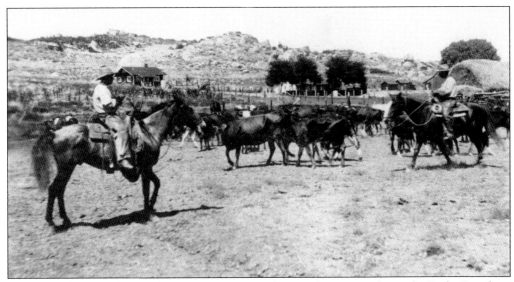

Albert "Zeke" Reed (left) and Isaac Parks (right) are rounding up cattle on the Parks Ranch in the 1940s just before the ranch was to be sold. The ranch property and the entire Parks Valley is now known as Lake Riverside Estates. (Courtesy of Mary E. Parks.)

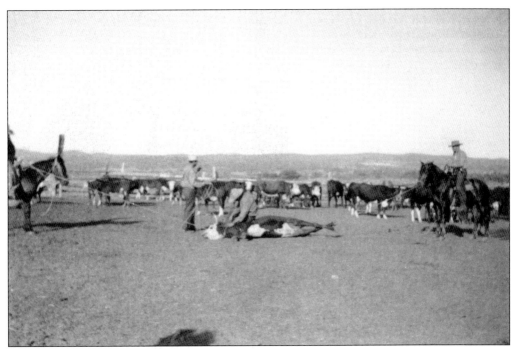

Cattle branding was a difficult chore. First it took considerable skill by two ropers to get the animal roped by both the head and the heels. Then it was thrown to the ground so it could be branded. In this photograph, the rope is being removed from this recently branded cow. (Courtesy of Clarena Dennis.)

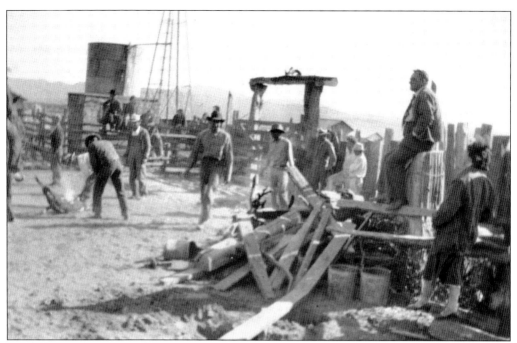

Cattle branding meant a day of dust, dirt, blood, and good food. There was also plenty of free advice from fence-sitting experts. The host ranch whose cattle were being branded always provided a hardy meal to those helping with the work. The tall man with the hat, walking toward the camera, is Lincoln Hamilton. (Courtesy of Clarena Dennis.)

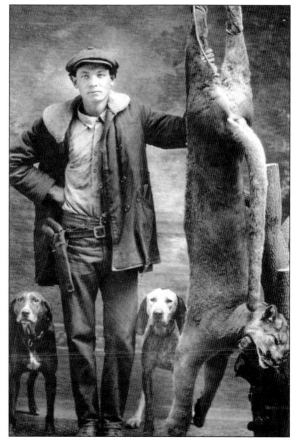

The ranchers who depended on cattle for their livelihood waged a continuous battle with predatory animals that preyed on their cattle. Hunting and trapping of mountain lions and coyotes was necessary to keep them under control. In 1920, nineteen-year-old Jim Wellman used his hounds to track down and bag this lion that had been destroying the family's cattle. (Courtesy of the Hamilton Museum Collection.)

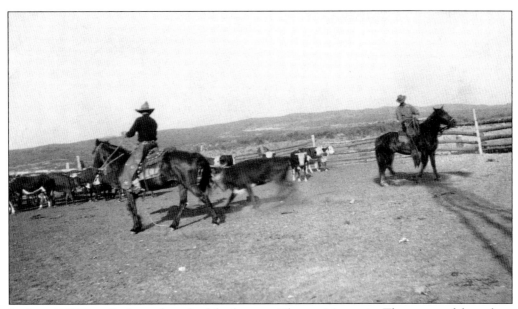

In the mid-1920s, a fire burned much of the forest on Thomas Mountain. The resourceful ranchers in the area used the fire-damaged cedar and pine trees to build fences, sheds, and corrals, such as these used in a pole corral in Anza. (Courtesy of Bud and Bobbie Wellman.)

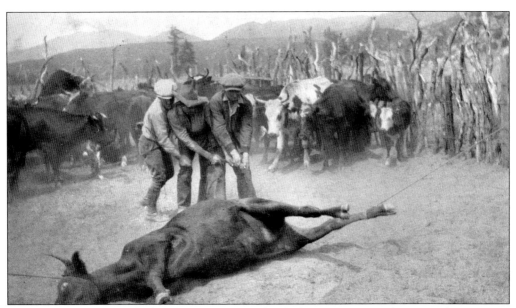

Even after being roped by the head and heels, it took three men to get this animal in position to brand. Note how the Arnaiz family made use of the native brush poles to make the corral at their Kenworthy Ranch. (Courtesy of Bud and Bobbie Wellman.)

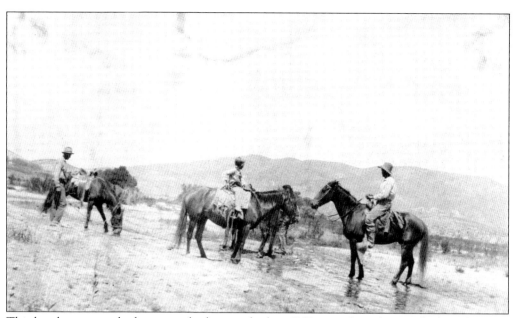

This break to water the horses took place in the late 1920s on a long, hot cattle drive from the hills to the railroad cattle yards in Temecula where the animals were taken for sale. The riders are, from left to right, unidentified, eight-year-old Bud Wellman, and Jim Wellman. (Courtesy of Bud and Bobbie Wellman.)

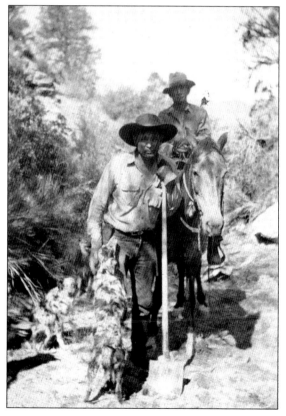

The area cattle ranchers were among the first conservationists, keeping springs and water holes in good condition for the native wildlife as well as for their cattle. In the 1930s, Jim Wellman (shovel in hand) and Ernest Arnaiz are returning from working on a spring in the Pinyon Flats area. The ranchers kept many of the trails open; they were also used by hikers, prospectors, and others. (Courtesy of Bud and Bobbie Wellman.)

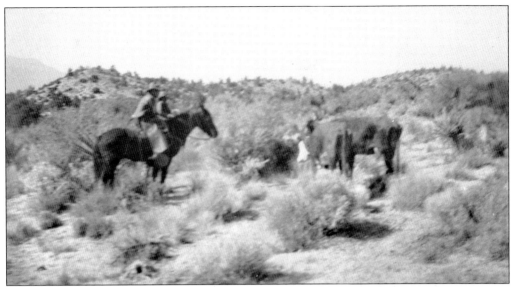

Cattle sometimes wandered off and over a time, sometimes years, would turn wild in the remote and rough canyons and valleys. If caught, they were difficult to handle. When cattle became wild, such as these two, they were either necked (tied) together or necked to a burro in order to make it easier to get them back to where they should be. (Courtesy of Bud and Bobbie Wellman.)

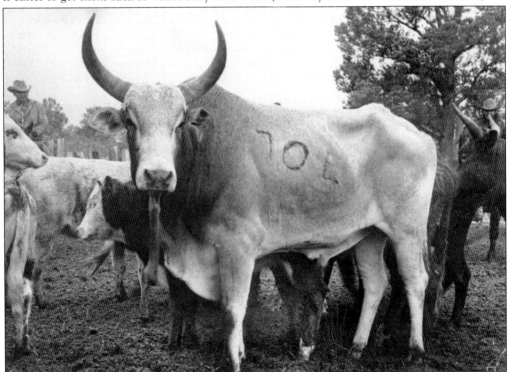

After missing for three or four years, this Brahma steer with the "7OL" brand, belonging to Jim Wellman, was located with another herd of cattle in Ebens Valley near Santa Rosa Mountain. Getting the steer to leave the herd he had been with for three or four years proved to be a difficult task. (Courtesy of Bud and Bobbie Wellman.)

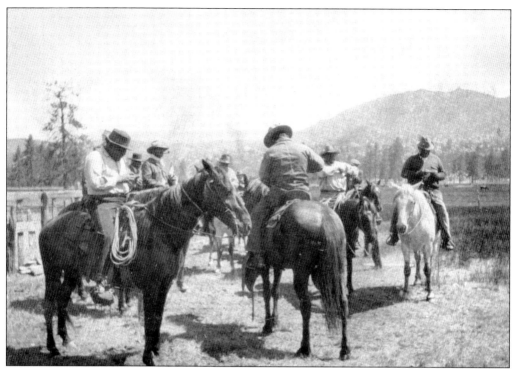

Cattlemen from the Cahuilla and Santa Rosa Indian Reservations and ranchers from the surrounding areas all helped each other in gathering the cattle for branding, sorting by owner, and shipping. This photograph, taken in the early 1900s, shows friends and neighbors ready for a day of riding at the Hamilton Ranch in Kenworthy. (Courtesy of Bud and Bobbie Wellman.)

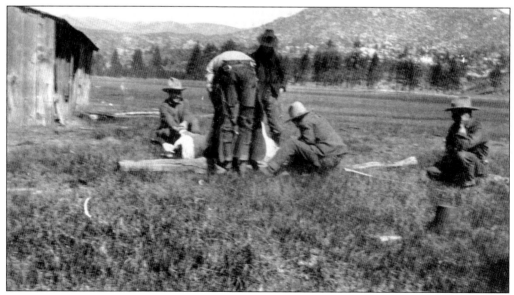

Ranch families did their own butchering when meat was needed for the table. Here the animal is being butchered right on the ground. The more common procedure was to have the animal hanging from a tree to remove the hide and to butcher it. (Courtesy of the Hamilton Museum Collection.)

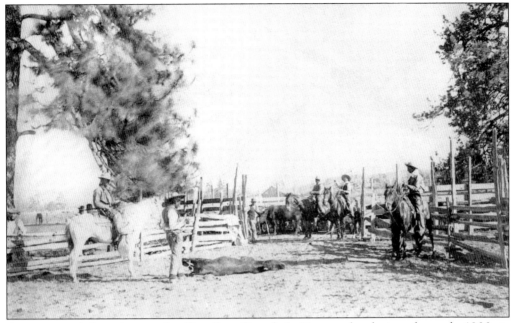

Assisting with branding at the Hamilton Ranch in Kenworthy during the early 1900s is Henry Hamilton, standing at the back of the animal lying on the ground; all the others are unidentified. The animal has been roped by its head and its heels. (Courtesy of the Hamilton Museum Collection.)

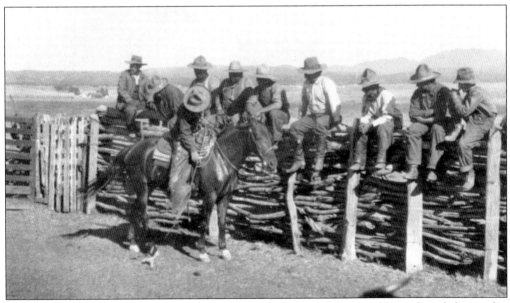

Taking a break on the fence after helping at the Parks Ranch are neighbors, from left to right, Mateo Caserro, Pat Caserro, three unidentified men, Henry Bergman, Buck Davidson, Sal Biles, and Gib Davidson. On horseback is Gib Reed. (Courtesy Mary E. Parks.)

Four

HOMESTEADS

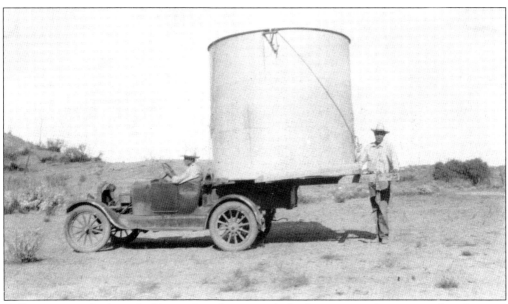

Sufficient water for household use often determined whether or not a farmer stayed in the area. In the 1920s, Jim Wellman (driving) and Lincoln Hamilton brought this storage tank from Los Angeles for water storage. Until 1949, when the first deep irrigation well was dug, most farming in the hills was done by dry farming, meaning crops were raised without irrigation. (Courtesy of the Hamilton Museum Collection.)

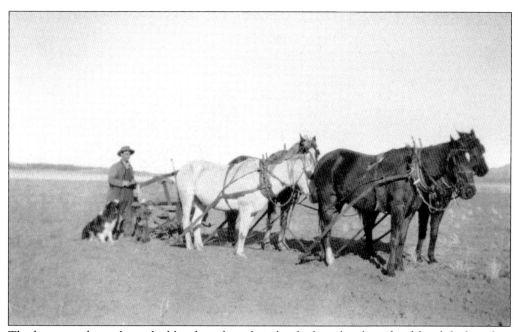

The homestead people worked hard to clear their land of sagebrush and redshank before they could even start to plow and plant. After the fields were plowed, as seen in this photograph, and planted, there was still no guarantee that there would be a harvest. It all depended on rain and whether it came at the right time and in the right amount. (Courtesy of the Hamilton Museum Collection.)

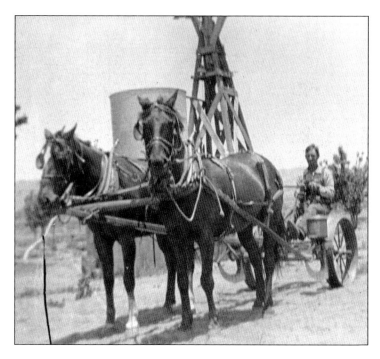

Well into the 1930s and 1940s, much of the farm work was done with horses or mules rather than with motorized equipment. Here, around 1912, John Contreras drives past the windmill and water storage tank at the Contreras homestead with his team of horses, Buster and Peter, ready for a day of planting. (Courtesy of the Hamilton Museum Collection.)

Calistro Tortes of the Santa Rosa Indian Reservation was well known for his vegetables and fruit, especially the apples that he grew. The apples were from trees planted by Tortes's ancestor, Manuel Torte, from seedlings that had been given to him by Manuel Arnaiz. Here is Tortes at Santa Rosa in the 1940s digging potatoes grown in his large garden. (Courtesy of Robert Tyler.)

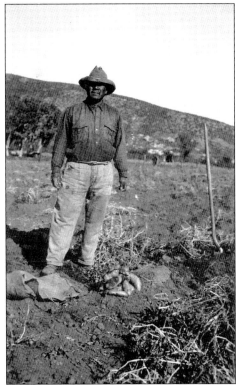

With good weather and adequate rainfall at the right time, this hay grew enough to be cut and baled. A baling crew and the baler usually moved from one ranch to another to harvest the hay. Note the bales of hay coming out just to the right of the third man from the left. (Courtesy of the Hamilton Museum Collection.)

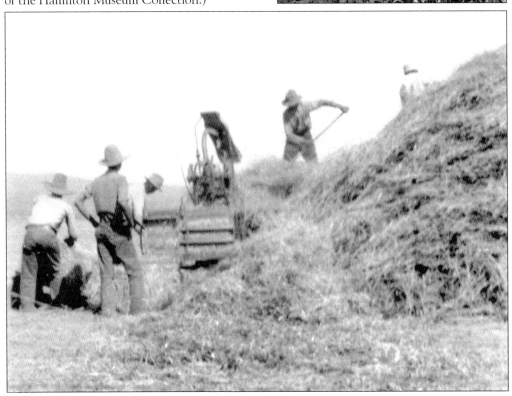

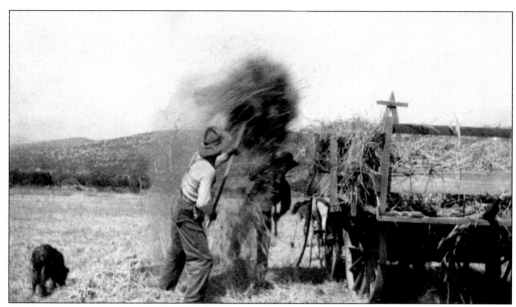

If the weather was not cooperative, resulting in a poor hay crop, the hay was not baled. Instead, it was left in the field for livestock to eat or was cut and stored loose in stacks or in a barn. Here, in 1909, men at Isaac Parks's ranch pitch hay into a wagon in preparation for winter at what is now Lake Riverside Estates. (Courtesy of Mary E. Parks.)

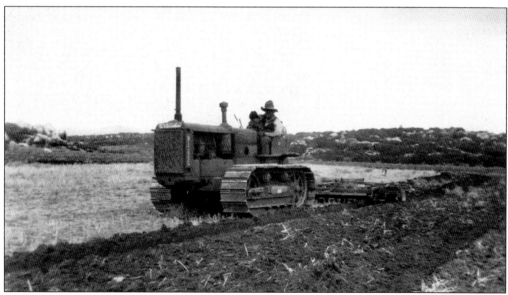

William Bradford was one of the first men in the hills to be appointed justice of the peace after the formation of Riverside County in 1893. Bradford farmed on his homestead near Parks Valley to the west of Cahuilla Indian Reservation. Here, in 1939, Bill Bradford, a relative on William's new diesel tractor, carries on the family farming tradition. (Courtesy of Barbara Bradford.)

A deep well dug in 1949 by Lincoln Hamilton was the beginning of a complete change in the way crops were grown. With irrigation, gladiolas, potatoes, sugar-beet seed, alfalfa, and alfalfa seed were grown. Here, in the 1950s, Hamilton stands in one of his first sugar-beet fields just before harvesting the seed. (Courtesy of the Hamilton Museum Collection.)

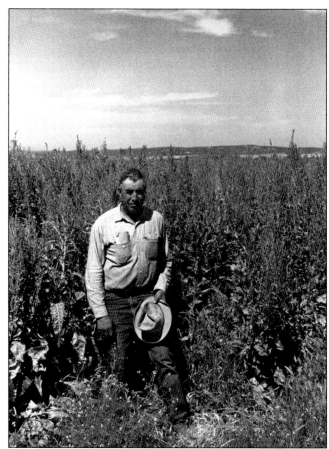

Lincoln Hamilton (standing), with an unidentified assistant on the tractor, is harvesting a seed crop in the 1950s from an irrigated field. The gathering apparatus attached to this tractor vacuumed up the seed. Hamilton often adapted or manufactured farming equipment to meet his own special needs. (Courtesy of the Hamilton Museum Collection.)

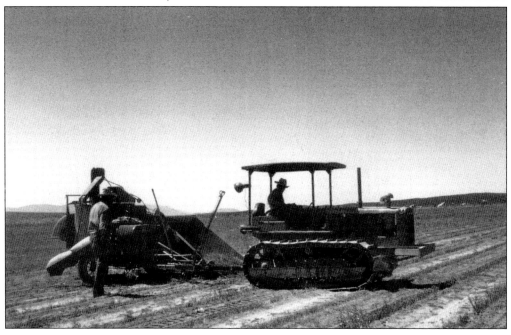

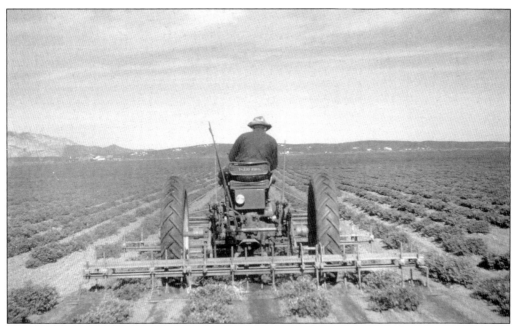

Lincoln Hamilton is pictured in 1949 cultivating one of his various irrigated crops, probably alfalfa, using a tractor with a tilling attachment. Hamilton used them to loosen the soil for irrigation, rid the fields of weeds, and maintain the quality of his seed crops. (Courtesy of the Hamilton Museum Collection.)

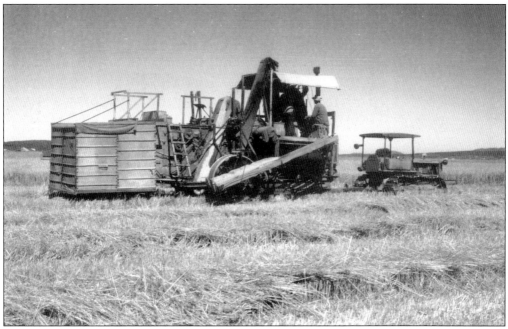

This 1949 photograph illustrates Lincoln Hamilton's threshing machine used to separate grain from the stalk in this dry-farmed oat field. The threshing machine was used to harvest various grains, such as rye, wheat, oats, and barley grown in both irrigated and dry-farmed fields. (Courtesy of the Hamilton Museum Collection.)

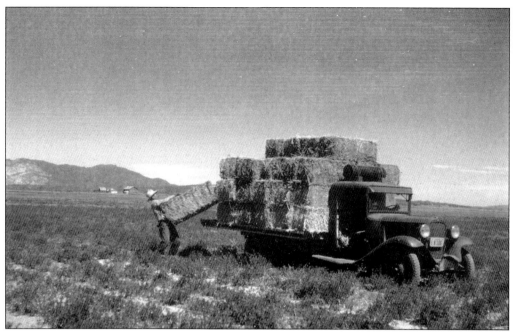

By 1955, Lincoln Hamilton was growing alfalfa hay in irrigated fields that would be loaded onto trucks by hand. Hamilton also raised alfalfa for seed, which had to be certified to be sold. (Courtesy of the Hamilton Museum Collection.)

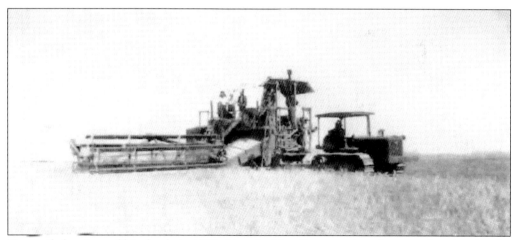

Up until the time of his death in 1976, Lincoln Hamilton continued to use this thresher he had adapted for his special needs to harvest both irrigated and dry-farmed grain crops. In this photograph, Hamilton is harvesting a dry-farmed barley crop. (Courtesy of the Hamilton Museum Collection.)

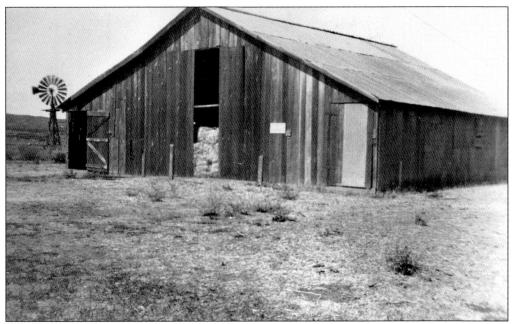

John and Fanny Contreras built this barn soon after 1910 when they filed on 160 acres of homestead land in Anza Valley. The barn is still standing and remains on the homestead property where the Hamilton Museum operates today. The wood siding of the barn has been replaced with metal. (Courtesy of the Hamilton Museum Collection.)

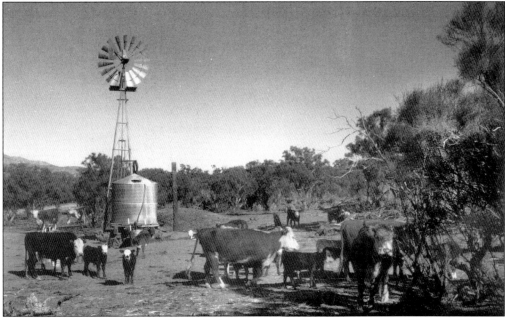

Water was very important for all people living in the hill country. The ranchers needed it for their livestock and household use. Homestead people needed water not just for home use, but also for their animals, gardens, and fruit trees if possible. Since Anza has always had a good strong breeze, windmills and a storage tank were the usual solution for ensuring that water was available. (Courtesy of the Hamilton Museum Collection.)

Five

FAMILIES

James Hamilton (1821–1897), a man of mixed ancestry, arrived in the valley in the 1870s with his children Mary, Joe, Henry, and Frank. Highly respected in the area, he spent his life as a rancher running his cattle across the entire valley, down into Coyote Canyon, and over in the meadows at Kenworthy. He was greatly saddened by the murder of his youngest son, Frank, in 1895. (Courtesy of the Hamilton Museum Collection.)

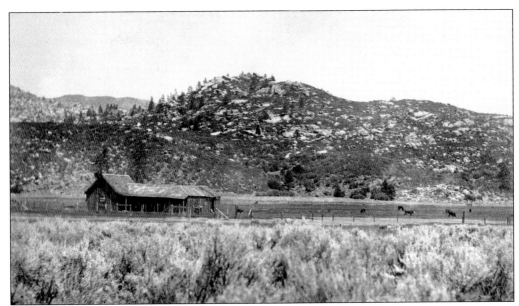

The Hamilton home in Kenworthy continued to be used by members of the family until the mid-1920s. James Hamilton's son Joe and wife, Clara Arnaiz Wellman, raised their four children and Clara's two children in this house. Later in the 1920s, Clara's son, Jim Wellman, lived in the house with his young family. (Courtesy of the Hamilton Museum Collection.)

Joe Hamilton (1857–1927) was James Hamilton's oldest son. He and his first wife, Rosadia Powett, were the parents of Augustine Hamilton. Joe's second wife was Clara Arnaiz, the widow of Frank Wellman. Joe and Clara Hamilton became the parents of Lincoln, Agnes, Lucy, and Frank, known as "Gummy." (Courtesy of the Hamilton Museum Collection.)

Frank Hamilton (1861–1895), James Hamilton's youngest son, was a highly respected Riverside County constable. He was shot and killed in San Jacinto by Charley Marshall. Marshall was tried and sentenced to hang, but the sentence was overturned on a technicality, and he was then sent to prison. Marshall was later paroled to the Garner Ranch in the San Bernardino Mountains where he spent his remaining years. (Courtesy of the Hamilton Museum Collection.)

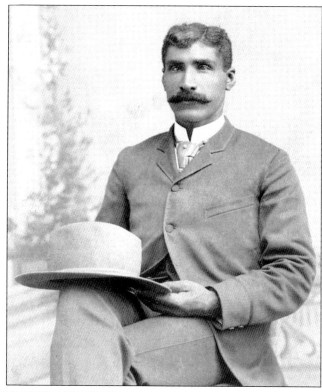

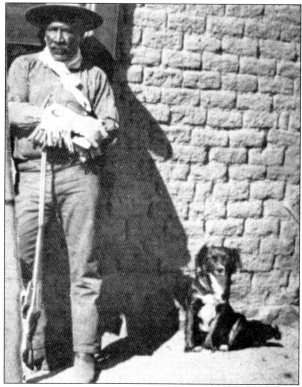

Henry Hamilton (1859–1933,) an older brother of Frank, attended the murder trial of his brother's killer and wrote almost daily from Riverside to his sister, Mary Hamilton, keeping her updated on the proceedings. Like his father, James, and older brother Joe Henry was a cattleman his entire life. (Courtesy of the Hamilton Museum Collection.)

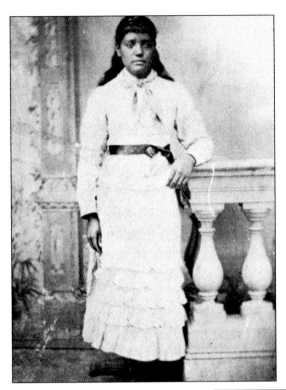

Mary Hamilton (1854–1899) was James Hamilton's eldest child. In addition to the daily correspondence she received from her brother Henry reporting on the trial proceedings of Frank's murder, she was an avid letter writer and received many a correspondence from others throughout her life. (Courtesy of the Hamilton Museum Collection.)

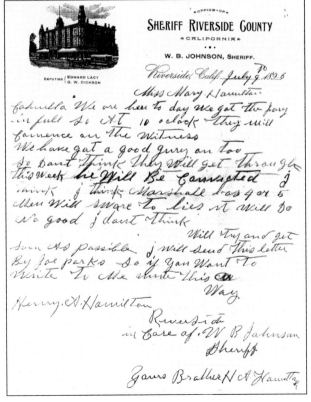

This is one of the letters from Henry to Mary regarding the trial of Charley Marshall for the murder of their brother Frank. Joe Parks, a friend, delivered the letter to Mary. Notice the official sheriff of Riverside County stationary. (Courtesy of the Hamilton Museum Collection.)

This is a letter dated April 28, 1895, from Lettie Lewis, a friend of Mary Hamilton, concerning the murder in San Jacinto of Mary's youngest brother Frank. (Courtesy of the Hamilton Museum Collection.)

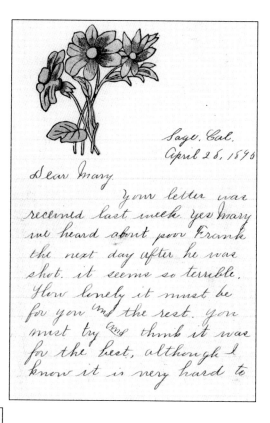

Sage, Cal.
April 28, 1895

Dear Mary
                Your letter was received last week. yes Mary we heard about poor Frank the next day after he was shot. it seems so terrible. How lonely it must be for you and the rest. you must try and think it was for the best, although I know it is very hard to

think so when we loose our dear ones. I can sympathize with you and I know how sad you feel for I lost a brother too. I hope the man who did the deed will be hung. he is trying very hard to get out. but if he does get out I hope the Cahuilla boys will get him and lynch him. Ma says to tell you that she feels very sorry for you all.
    Well we are having rainy weather to day. it was raining this morning

This is the second page of the Lewis letter to Mary Hamilton. Lettie Lewis wrote, "I hope the man who did the deed will be hung. He is trying very hard to get out, but if he does get out, I hope the Cahuilla boys will get him and lynch him." Marshall was later paroled to work at the Garner Ranch in the San Bernardino Mountains. (Courtesy of the Hamilton Museum Collection.)

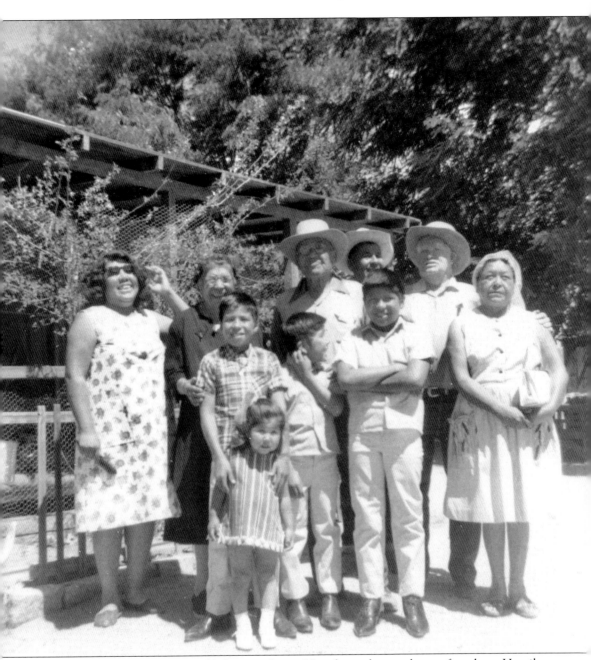

Frank Hamilton's great-grandfather was James Hamilton, the gentleman for whom Hamilton School was named. Frank grandparents were Joe and Rosadia Powett Hamilton and his parents were Augustine and Caroline Apapas Hamilton. These are the family and friends of Frank and Anne Tortes Hamilton. Pictured are, from left to right, (first row) Joe Hamilton, with his hands on Rose Anne's shoulders; Manuel Hamilton; and James "Pancho" Hamilton; (second row) Anne Tortes Hamilton, Rosinda Lubo, Frank Hamilton, Lupe Lubo, Bill Bradford, and Rosalie Valencia. The Hamilton family continues to be very active in the community. (Courtesy of Barbara Bradford.)

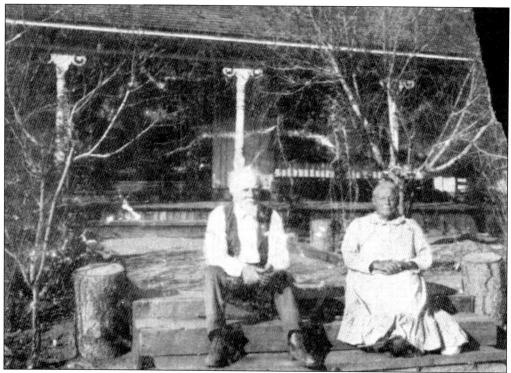

In the 1860s, Charley and Genoveva Bardico Thomas settled in Hemet Valley, now called Garner Valley, just across the valley from where Lake Hemet Dam was built in the 1890s. The Thomases were known for their fine horses and Durham cattle. Thomas Mountain was named for the family and the valley around the Thomas Ranch was soon being called Thomas Valley. (Courtesy of the Hamilton Museum Collection.)

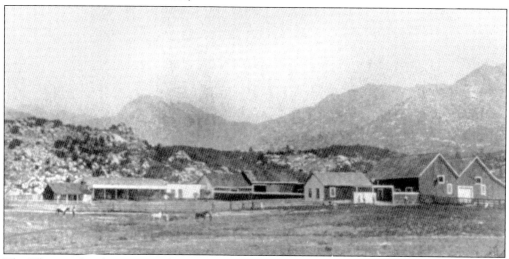

The Thomas family continued to improve the ranch and lived on the property until about 1909, when they sold everything to Robert Garner. Thomas Valley then became known as Garner Valley. It was not until the 1970s that the southern end of the valley, Hemet Valley or Kenworthy, was subdivided and then also called Garner Valley. (Courtesy of the Hamilton Museum Collection.)

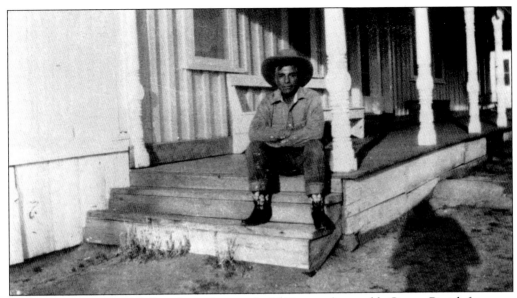

For many years, Horace McGee, shown here in the 1940s, was the capable Garner Ranch foreman, managing the large Garner cattle operation from Lake Hemet to the junction of State Highways 74 and 371. (Courtesy of Bud and Bobbie Wellman.)

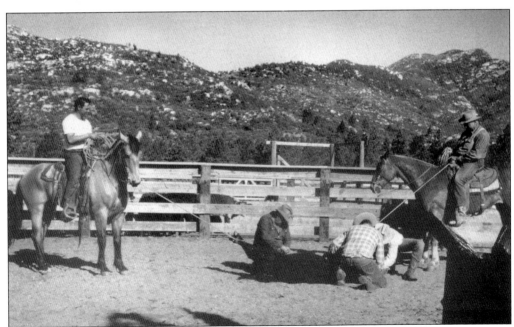

As was the custom when there was ranch work to be done, the neighboring ranchers helped each other. Here, in the 1960s, cattlemen from Anza and the Cahuilla and Santa Rosa Indian Reservations help out with branding at the Garner Ranch. Some of the Garner family continues to live on a part of the original Thomas land. (Courtesy of the Hamilton Museum Collection.)

In the 1860s, the Reed and Parks families came to California in covered wagons from Texas looking for a place to settle with their cattle. Naoma and Asa Reed, seen here, settled to the west of Cahuilla Mountain in what is now Reed Valley. David and Frances Parks settled to the west of the Cahuilla Indian Reservation in what is now Lake Riverside. (Courtesy of Mary E. Parks.)

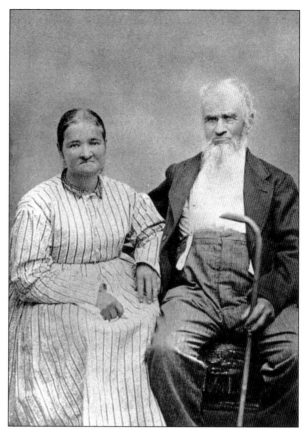

Quitman Reed, a son of Asa and Naoma Reed, ranched on the west side of Cahuilla Mountain. This picture of Quitman Reed and his sister Frances Reed Parks was taken in 1911. He married Edith Tripp, a member of the pioneer Tripp family in Tripp Flats. Their sons, Albert (Zeke), Lester, and Gib, were all active cattlemen. Lester also wrote books about the area. (Courtesy of Mary E. Parks.)

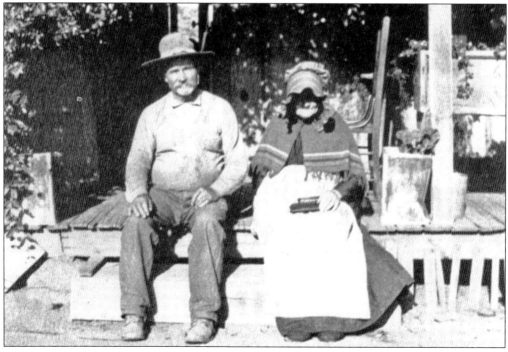

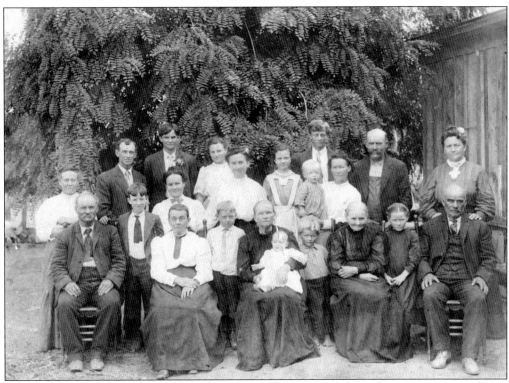

Here Frances Parks and several of her siblings pose in the early 1900s. Frances and several other members of the Parks family are buried on the old ranch property now called Lake Riverside. (Courtesy of Mary E. Parks.)

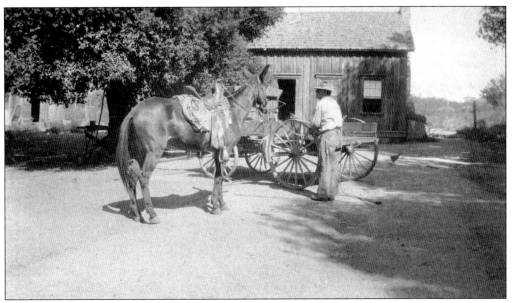

Jay Parks, son of David and Frances Parks, and his mule are seen here at the William Bradford Ranch in the early 1900s. Other Parks children were Joseph Quitman Parks, Elizabeth "Lizzie" Parks, Isaac "Ike" Parks, Lucy Narcissus Parks, and Lincoln Parks. (Courtesy of Barbara Bradford.)

Teresa de Monroy Arnaiz, who was born in Valparaiso, Spain, in 1830, arrived in San Francisco sometime before 1856 after making the voyage with her husband, Eugenio, around Cape Horn and South America in a sailing ship. She later lived in Kenworthy with her son Manuel and his family at their homestead. (Courtesy of the Hamilton Museum Collection.)

Teresa de Monroy Arnaiz died in 1893 during very wet weather. The rain damaged the dirt roads so much Arnaiz's body could not be transported to San Jacinto for burial, making it necessary for her to be buried at the family homestead. The Thomas, Hamilton, and Wellman families helped the Arnaiz family make a casket from the Arnaiz barn before burying her nearby. (Courtesy of the Hamilton Museum Collection.)

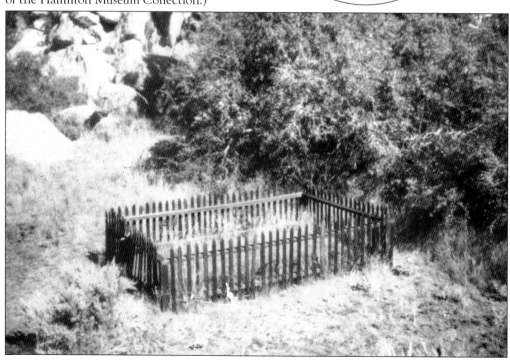

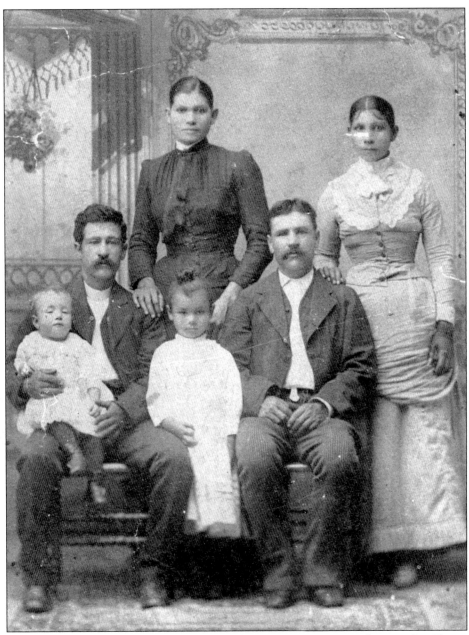

Manuel Arnaiz, the son of Eugenio and Teresa de Monroy Arnaiz, was born in San Francisco. As a very young man, he ventured south while working at ranches along the way. After Manuel's arrival in Colton, he met and married Dolores Garduna. They lived there for a time and then moved to Yucaipa, where Manuel again became interested in ranching. In 1886, while living in Yucaipa, Manuel and Dolores (the couple on the left) and their two children, Gene and Clara, sat for this photograph. Two more Arnaiz children, Daisy and Fanny, were born in Yucaipa. The couple on the right is Dolores's brother-in-law and sister, Gregorio and Manuela Quintana of Colton. By 1892, the young Arnaiz family, moved to the lush meadows at Kenworthy with their cattle. After the family's arrival in Kenworthy, four more sons, Dan, Ed, Ernest, and Henry, were born at the family homestead. (Courtesy of the Hamilton Museum Collection.)

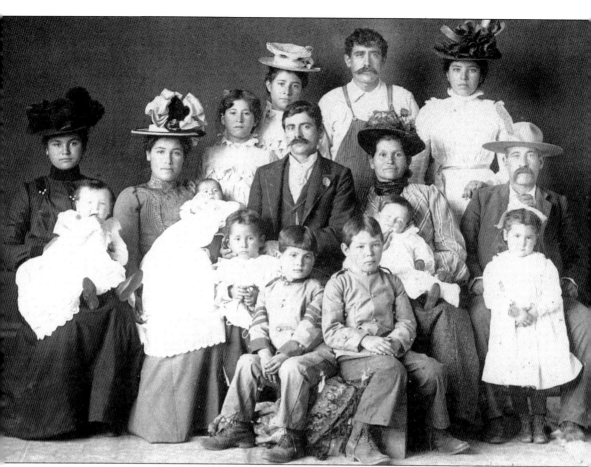

Members of the Wellman and Arnaiz family and several unidentified friends pose in 1901. Standing in the back next to an unidentified couple are Fanny (left) and Daisy Arnaiz; seated to the far left is Clara Arnaiz Wellman holding baby son Jim; and seated second from the right is Dolores Arnaiz, holding Henry, and to the right of her Manuel Arnaiz with Mary Wellman in front. Three of the younger Arnaiz sons, Ernest, Dan, and Ed, are clustered in front from left to right. Clara, Daisy, and Fanny are all daughters of Manuel and Dolores Arnaiz. Missing in this photograph of the family is the eldest son, Gene. (Courtesy of the Hamilton Museum Collection.)

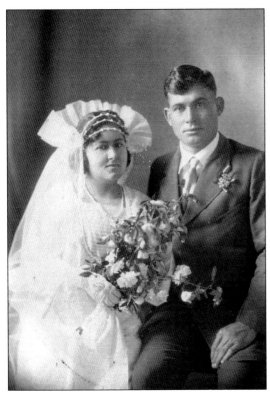

Ed, the son of Manuel and Dolores Arnaiz, was born and raised in Kenworthy. After his marriage to Beatrice Vega (left), the couple lived in Anza raising their four children, Eleanor, Abie, Gilbert, and Arnold. Ed also had a son, Angelo, with his first wife. All four sons were in the service during World War II; the first to serve was Angelo (below). (Courtesy of the Hamilton Museum Collection.)

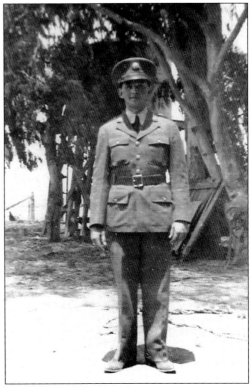

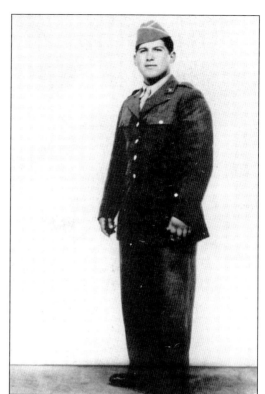

Ed and Beatrice Arnaiz's oldest son, Abie (right), served in the army in Europe during World War II. Another son, Gilbert (below), and his younger brother Arnold, were also in the service during World War II. Abie was the only one of the four Arnaiz sons to lose his life during the war. He was buried in Europe. (Courtesy of the Hamilton Museum Collection.)

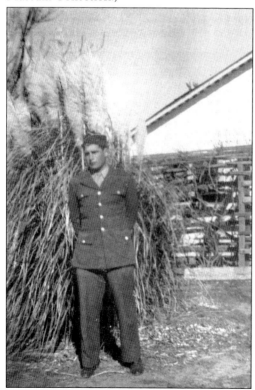

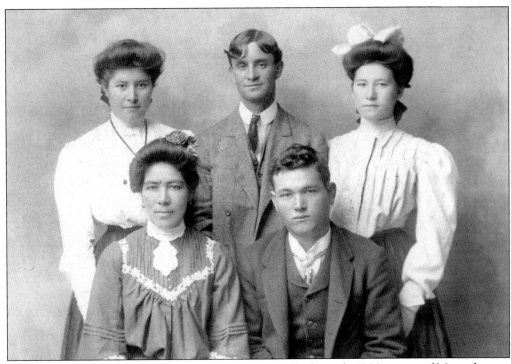

In the early 1900s, some of Manuel and Dolores Arnaiz's children pose with two of the children's spouses. Pictured from left to right are (first row) Virginia Estudillo Arnaiz and Gene Arnaiz; (second row) Daisy Arnaiz Contreras and John and Fanny Arnaiz Contreras. (Courtesy of the Hamilton Museum Collection.)

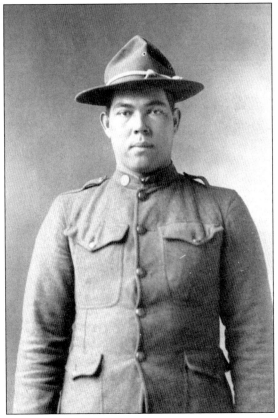

During times of war, many hill and mountain men performed their patriotic duty as servicemen. Among those serving overseas during World War I was Dan Arnaiz, son of Manuel and Dolores Arnaiz. (Courtesy of the Hamilton Museum Collection.)

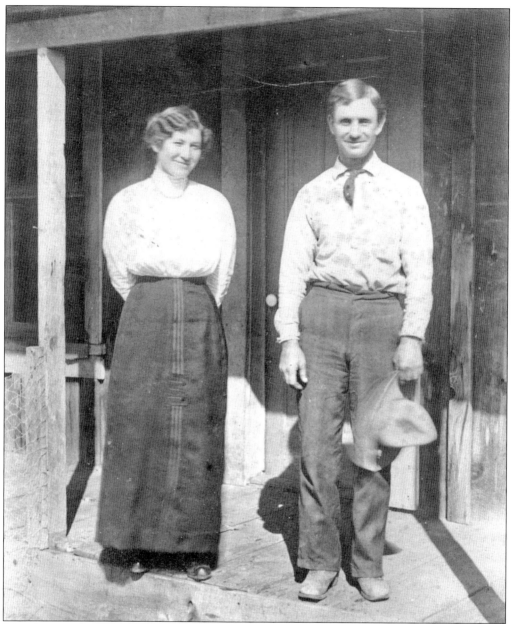

John Contreras and Fanny Arnaiz, the daughter of early Kenworthy settlers Manuel and Dolores Arnaiz, were married at her parent's home in Kenworthy in July 1906 by Judge William Vawters of San Jacinto. When land was reopened for homesteading on the Cahuilla Plains (Anza) in 1909, John and Fanny were among the first to file a claim. (Courtesy of the Hamilton Museum Collection.)

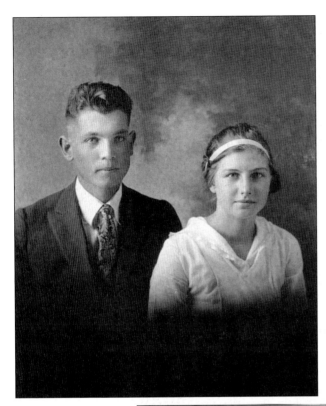

Jim Wellman, the son of Frank and Clara Arnaiz Wellman and grandson of Manuel and Dolores Arnaiz, married Elma Hall of Anza in 1920. The ceremony was performed by Judge William Bradford at the Bradford Ranch just west of Anza Valley and the Cahuilla Indian Reservation. The couple traveled by horse and buggy to the ceremony. Three children, Bud, Margaret, and Clarena, were born to this family. (Courtesy of the Hamilton Museum Collection.)

Lloyd and Jane Lubo Clarke were residents of the Cahuilla Indian Reservation. Jane's family, the Lubos, is one of the oldest Cahuilla families. Lloyd Clarke was a Hualapai Indian from Peach Springs, Arizona. Their grandson, Gerald Clarke, a well-known Cahuilla artist, now resides in Lloyd and Jane's original home. (Courtesy of Barbara Bradford.)

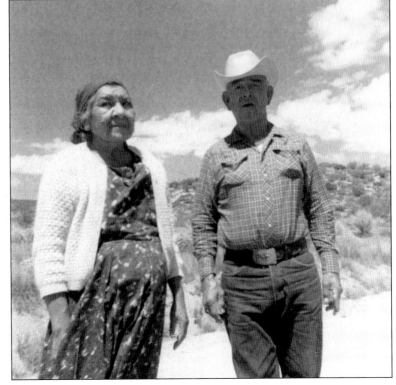

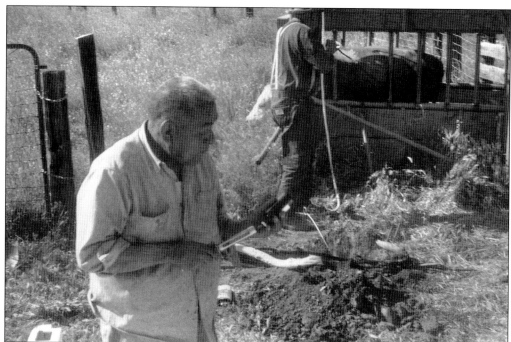

The Costos are known as an industrious, college-educated family. Some of the occupations they enjoyed were nursing, education, and music. Domingo Costo, seen above and at right, and Sylvester and Gilbert "Skip" Costo were successful cattlemen, who in addition to tending their own herds helped other cattlemen needing assistance. Domingo Costo spent several years in Hawaii assisting a resort owner with his horses. Sylvester and Skip were among area residents who served this country in the military. Sylvester was also a capable and patient Hamilton School bus driver and transported Anza area students to high school in Hemet; Skip was also a talented musician. Rupert Costo was one of the first Anza Electric Co-Op presidents, an educator, and a well-known Native American historian. (Courtesy of Barbara Bradford.)

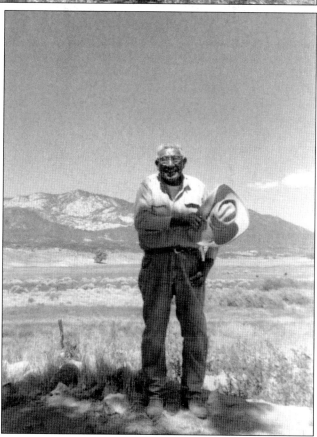

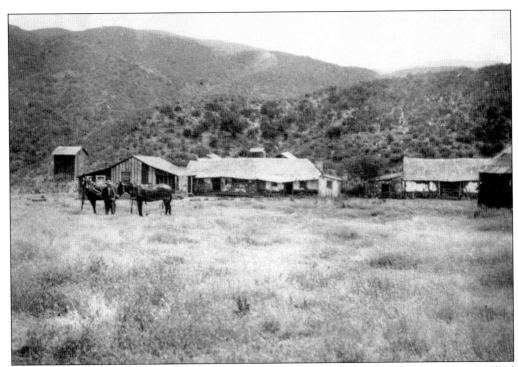

Jacob and Phillipena Bergman settled in the Aguanga area in the early 1800s on what was called the Mountain Ranch (above, around 1922); the ranch was also the site of the Butterfield Stage Station. When grown, one of the Bergman's sons, Henry, and his wife, Alice Godfrey, continued to live there raising their own family, including sons Arley and Harry. Arley and Annie Bergman and their family were cattle ranchers near the junction of State Highways 79 and 371. Harry and his wife, also named Alice, moved into this house (below) on the old dirt road between Aguanga and Anza in 1924. They continued to live there until they built a new adobe house in 1930 on the same property, where they raised their daughter Harriet. (Courtesy of Harriet Bergman Costo.)

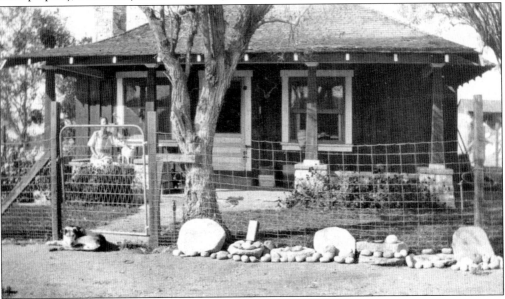

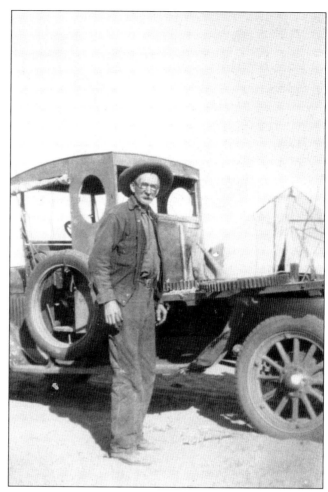

Frank and Fred Clark arrived in the valley around 1891. Frank (right) settled in Durazno Valley, a little place south of Anza and west of Terwilliger on the south side of the Cahuilla Indian Reservation. He married Annie Terwilliger, the daughter of Jacob and Almira Terwilliger. The Clarks raised their two children, Bud and Lola, at their cattle ranch in Durazno Valley. Below are, from left to right, Frank and Annie Clark with Doc Hopkins. Clark, a cattleman all his life, ran the livestock in the Terwilliger area and down to the desert floor around Borrego Springs. Clark lived in Durazno Valley until his death in 1937. (Courtesy of Mary Clark Garbani.)

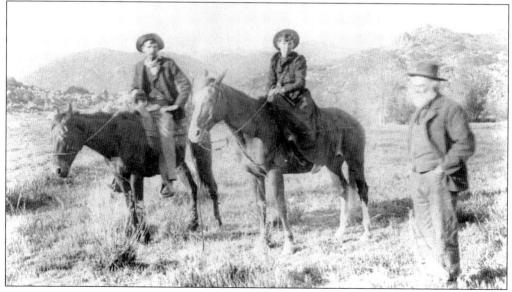

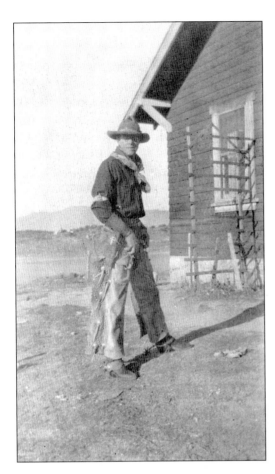

Bud Clark, at left, celebrates his 16th birthday wearing new cowboy gear and looking as if he might be a dude pretending to be a cowboy—maybe actor Tom Mix. Although he appears to be acting, Bud actually was a real ranch hand, assisting his father, Frank Clark, on his Durazno Valley ranch. In the photograph below, Bud appears in dressier attire. (Courtesy of Mary Clark Garbani.)

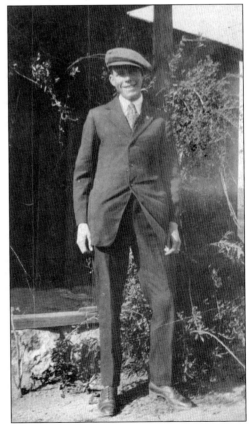

Fred Clark (right) was born in 1866 and arrived in the mountain area around 1891. He bought the property known as La Puerta Ranch in Terwilliger Valley. Fred, like his brother Frank, was a cattleman. The brothers ran their livestock down Coyote Canyon and onto the desert floor. Names on the desert area maps, like Clark Valley, Clark Dry Lake, and Clark Well, all remind people of these early cattlemen. In later years, Fred's interest turned more to horses rather than cattle; he was known for his well-trained animals. In the late 1930s, Fred sold his ranch to Art and Violet Cary. He died in San Jacinto in 1945. The property, now known as the Cary Ranch, is the site of a plaque commemorating the Juan Bautista de Anza expeditions of 1774–1775. In recent years, his small adobe house, seen below in the 1920s, has become just a pile of disintegrating adobe brick south of Coyote Canyon Road. (Courtesy Dick Cary.)

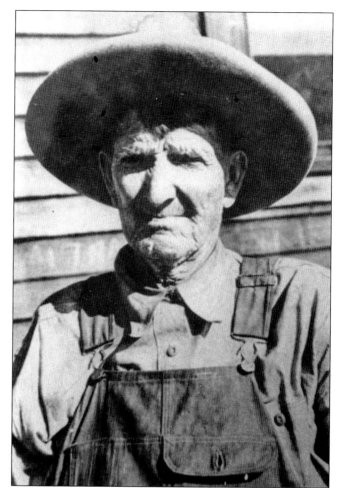

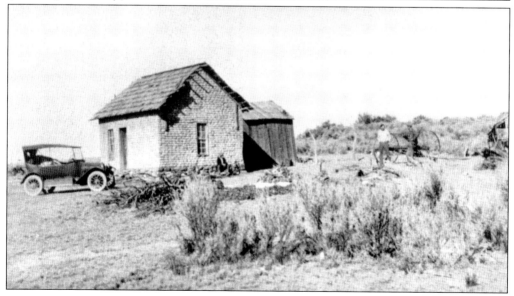

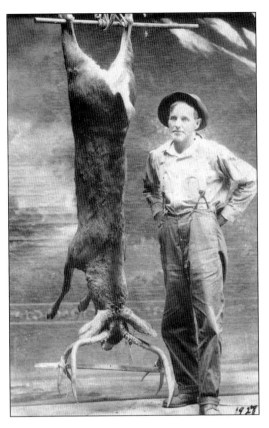

Around 1918, Ray Fobes and his wife, Maude, bought from George Spittler the mountain property known as Fobes Ranch above Garner Valley at the end of the current Fobes Road. As early as 1903, Ray was a stage driver carrying passengers and freight up and down the steep mountain roads between Idyllwild and Hemet. The Fobes became well known for their delicious mountain-grown pears, apples, and huge cabbages. However, their garden and orchard were a constant temptation to the deer population. At left, Ray proudly poses in this 1927 photograph taken not far from his garden with a large buck. The picture below is of Maude and Ray in the 1940s after they had sold their ranch and were caretakers at Lake Hemet. (Left, courtesy of Bud and Bobbie Wellman; below, courtesy of Clarena Dennis.)

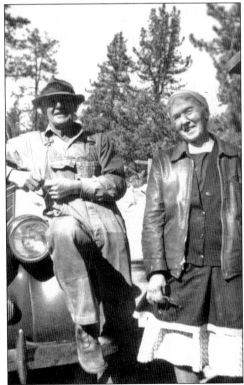

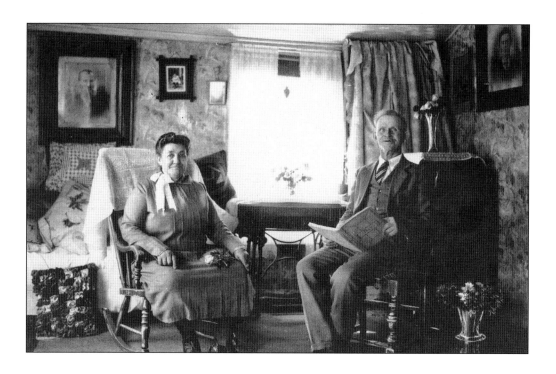

Noah and Alice Cary (above) and their family began homesteading around 1915 on the western side of the valley next to the Cahuilla Indian Reservation. The Cary children were all grown except for Art and Rose, who were the only ones in the family to attend Hamilton School. An older daughter, May, taught at Hamilton School for a short time. Several of the Cary offspring homesteaded land near their parent's property on Cary Road. By the early 1920s, Noah and Alice Cary had built this barn (below) and several outbuildings as well as their home. (Courtesy of Alice Hopkins and Dick Cary.)

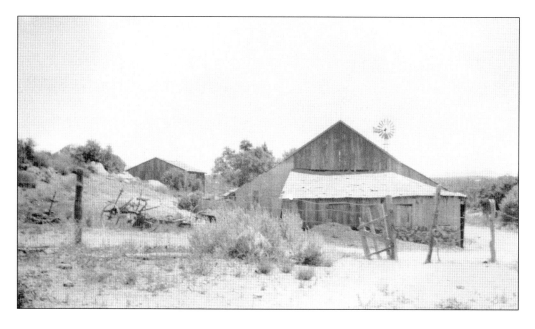

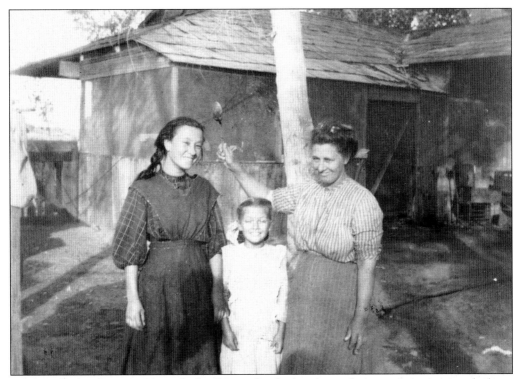

Noah and Alice Cary were mainly dry farmers but had some cattle, many fruit trees, and a large garden. Here, around 1915, daughters May and Rose and mother Alice take a break from farm chores. Rose spent her later life at the homestead and some of her descendants still occupy the property. (Courtesy Dick Cary.)

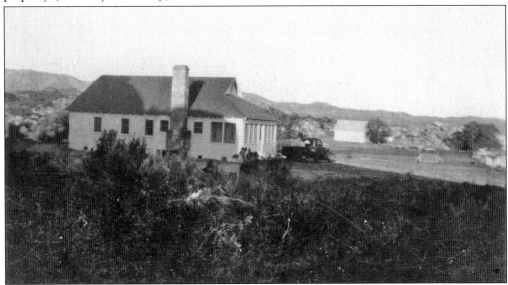

In the 1930s, Art Cary, son of Noah and Alice Cary, and his wife, Violet, moved to the Fred Clark Ranch in Terwilliger where they lived the rest of their lives. Art Cary's main occupation was raising horses and cattle and doing some dry farming. By 1941, they had built this house. (Courtesy Dick Cary.)

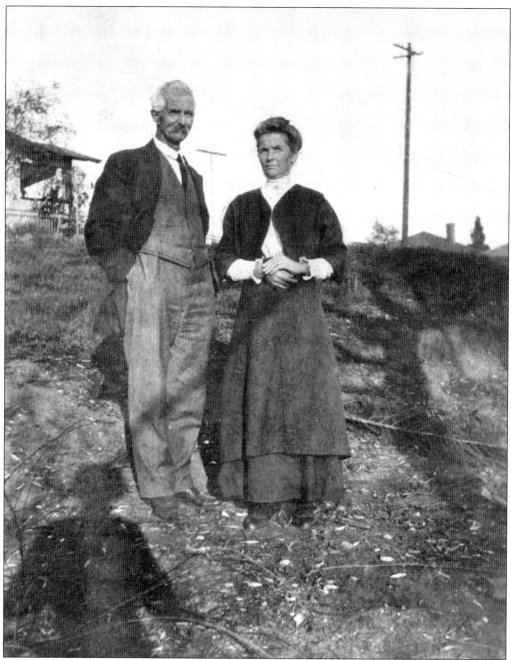

Carl and Alma Bahrman are shown here in 1916, the year they settled in Terwilliger Valley. As was quite usual when people filed on homestead property, Carl Bahrman continued to work in the city to support his family. Meanwhile, Alma and their five children worked on the land, clearing and planting, in order to meet the requirements to gain title on a homestead parcel. Two adult sons, Lincoln and Milton Bahrman, farmed and raised horses on their own property on Mitchell Road between Bautista and Bahrman Roads. Some of the Bahrman descendants continue to live on part of the original Bahrman homestead on Coyote Canyon Road in Terwilliger Valley. (Courtesy of Edell Lashley.)

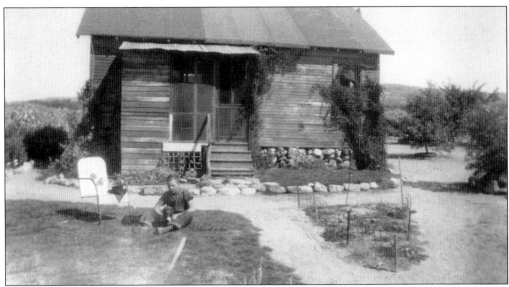

This is the original Carl and Alma Bahrman homestead house, built around 1918. Rollin Ford, grandson of Carl and Alma, is sitting in the front yard in 1944 after he and his parents, Ralph and Ella Bahrman Ford, moved to Anza. (Courtesy of Edell Lashley.)

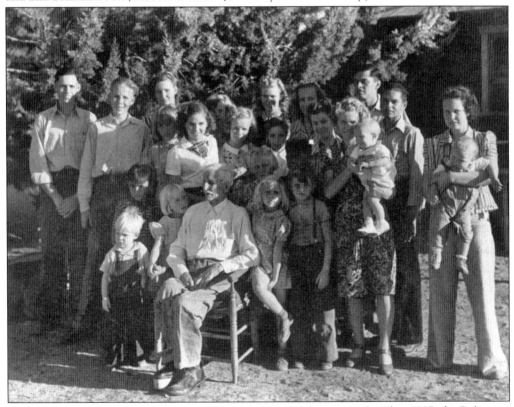

To celebrate the golden anniversary of Alma and Carl Bahrman in October 1937, the Bahrman family came together at the family home in Terwilliger Valley. Carl, in front in the chair, sits with some of his grandchildren and his first great-grandchild. (Courtesy of Edell Lashley.)

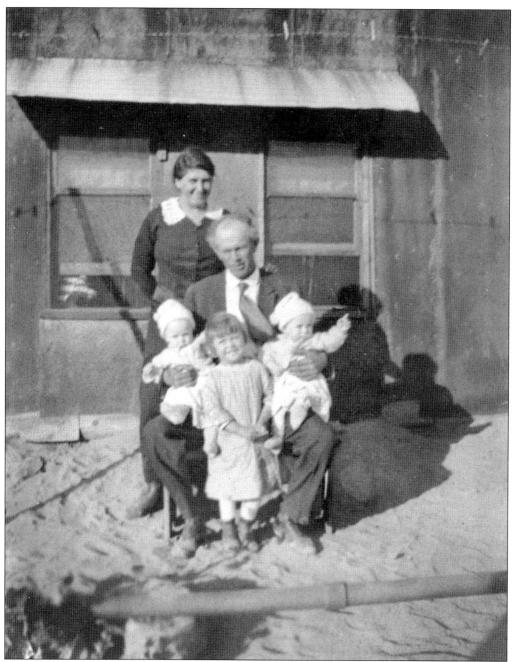

In the early 1900s, Fred Rapp had a plumbing business in the Los Angeles area. He accepted 80 acres of land here, in the Anza Valley, as payment for a plumbing bill. Rapp, his wife, and his young daughter moved to the valley with the intent of becoming farmers. While living there, his wife gave birth to two more children, twins, delivered at home with the aid of the Indian Agency doctor from the Cahuilla Indian Reservation. Rapp decided after a few years that he would rather be a plumber than a farmer and the Rapp family went back to the city and the plumbing business. The Fred Rapp family home was about where the Circle K is now. (Courtesy of the Hamilton Museum Collection.)

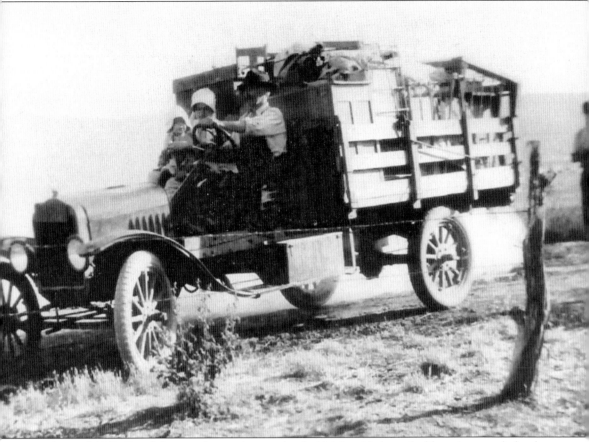

Around 1918, Ben Johnson, driving his truck piled high with household equipment, helped to move the belongings of James and Anna Bartlett to their homestead in Burnt Valley, just to the east of Anza Valley. Seated in the passenger side of the truck are Anna Hall Bartlett and her two children, Sidney and Betty. Her brother, Harry Hall, who had been a student at Hamilton School, is walking behind the truck. Other members of the Hall family to homestead in the valley in the early 1900s were Dan Hall and Elma Hall Wellman with her husband, Jim Wellman. (Courtesy of Roger and Alice Hall.)

Arthur and Lottie Hutton and small son James arrived in the north central part of the valley to homestead around 1918. To prove up (gain title) on their 160 acres, they cleared the land, planted crops, and built a typical homestead house. A windmill pumped water from a shallow well for household use and a team of horses, a milk cow, and a few chickens. (Courtesy of the Hamilton Museum Collection.)

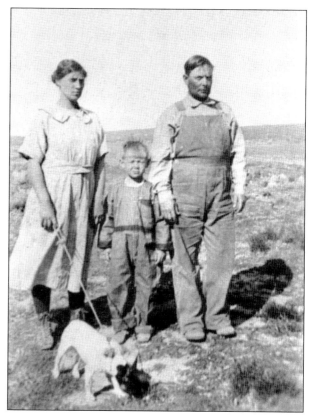

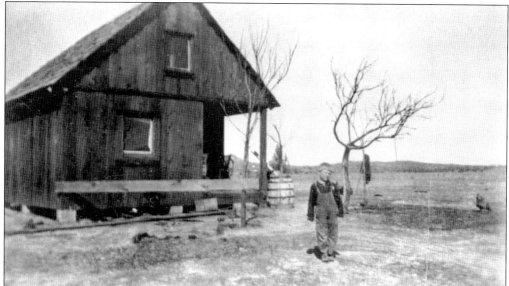

Note the hen and its enclosure in the foreground and the wooden rain barrel to the right of the Arthur Hutton home. Water was frequently in short supply if the wind did not blow the windmill enough. Prudent housewives kept a rain barrel under the eaves to catch water if it did rain. The rainwater was used for everything from washing one's hair to keeping a treasured plant alive. (Courtesy of the Hamilton Museum Collection.)

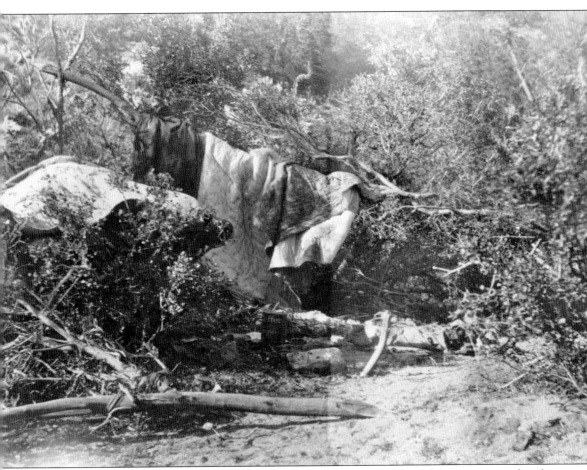

Heller Springs Road in Terwilliger is one road that was not named for a pioneer family. Instead, it was named for a killer by the name of Al Heller. In 1916, many homes in the valley and surrounding area were being robbed of food, clothing, and small tools. It was noted that an unfamiliar man was seen sneaking through the brush in Terwilliger near the Fred Clark Ranch. A posse consisting of Roy Tripp, Fred Clark, Henry Hamilton, and Ben Johnson was sent to the area to try and get to the bottom of the problem. When the man was found hiding in a primitive camp, he began shooting without warning and killed Roy Tripp, the son of the pioneer Tripp family. The posse fired several shots into the canvas shelter, killing Al Heller. A note found in Heller's pocket read, "This is Heller, tell my wife." In this 1930s picture, the tattered strips of rotting canvas, rusty tin cans, and other debris are still seen scattered about Heller's former camp. (Courtesy of the Hamilton Museum Collection.)

Six

EDUCATION

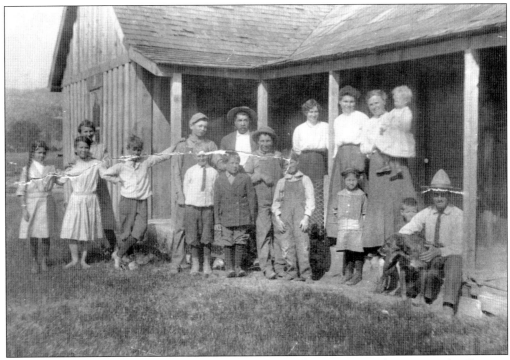

Education in the hills usually took place in barns or homes. For a short time, the Casners conducted a boarding school in Anza Valley. The Tripp families had a school at Tripp Flats. Later in the 1890s, a school was built at the short-lived mining town of Kenworthy. In this Kenworthy School photograph, taken around 1914, many pioneer families are represented. (Courtesy of the Hamilton Museum Collection.)

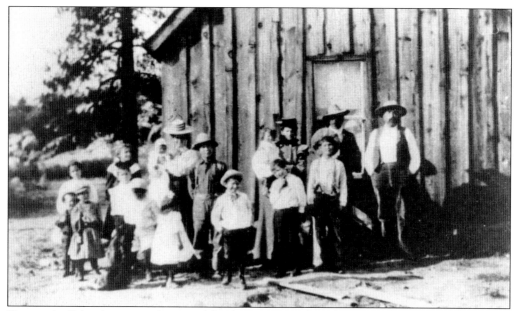

Kenworthy School continued to serve the mountain residents long after the town of Kenworthy disappeared. Lumber from the abandoned town found new use when it was used to build a home for the teacher and other buildings throughout the hills. Children attending Kenworthy School in the early 1900s were from families living in the surrounding area, including Anza and the Santa Rosa Indian Reservation. (Courtesy of the Hamilton Museum Collection.)

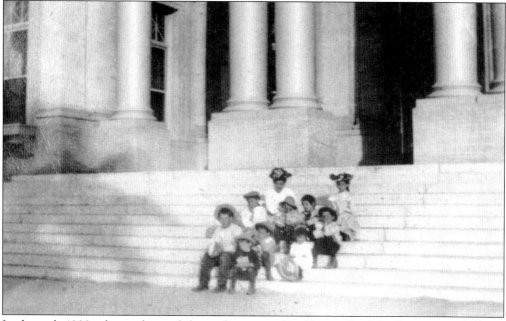

In the early 1900s, the teacher and the students attending Kenworthy School went on a field trip by covered wagon to Oceanside for the student's first view of the Pacific Ocean. After camping along the seashore for a few days, the travelers returned via Riverside, where they posed on the courthouse steps for this photograph before heading back to the mountains. (Courtesy of the Hamilton Museum Collection.)

In 1909, children attending the Kenworthy School and other one-room mountain schools had little or no playground equipment; many large boulders near the school often took the place of swings and slides. This group of students and their teacher seem quite happy with their "playground equipment." (Courtesy of the Hamilton Museum Collection.)

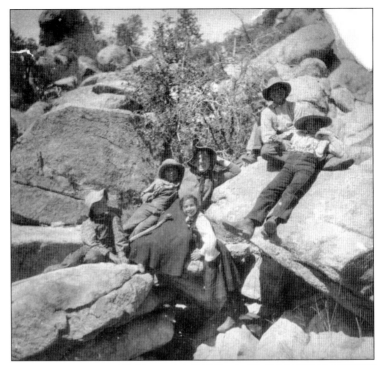

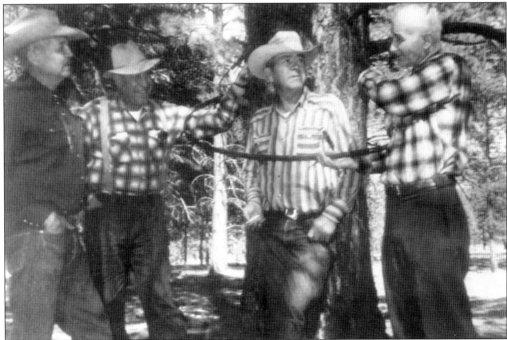

In 1910, these four men were young Kenworthy School pranksters who put a metal buggy wheel rim over the top of a young pine tree. Pictured here in 1963 from left to right are Jim Wellman, Lincoln Hamilton, Henry Arnaiz, and Joe Scherman as they stand beneath that same tree, now grown tall, and recall their struggle to get the rim over the top of the tree. (Courtesy of the Hamilton Museum Collection.)

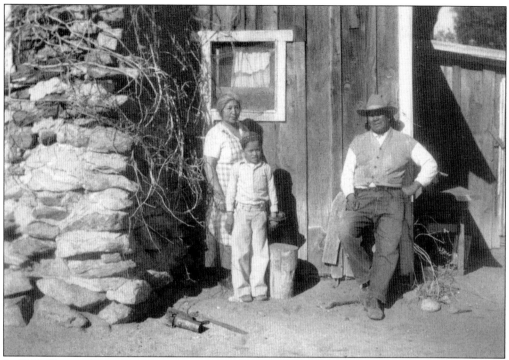

In 1933, Kenworthy Indian Emergency School was built near the junction of State Highways 371 and 74 for students living in Kenworthy and at the Santa Rosa Indian Reservation. First-grader George Tortes, pictured with his parents, Calistro and Vacilla, decided school was not for him. He hotfooted it, that is ran, seven miles home, arriving before the school bus. Eighth-grade graduates in 1936 at the Kenworthy Indian Emergency School were Audmer McKibben and Bud Wellman. (Courtesy of Robert Tyler.)

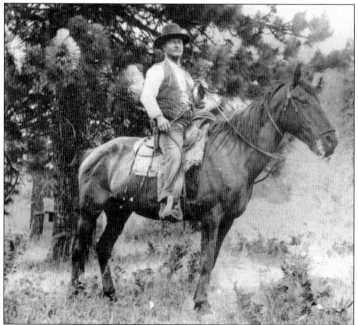

A school was needed in Anza, resulting in the formation of the Hamilton School District in 1913, but there was no schoolhouse. Joe G. (pictured) and Sofie Scherman offered their barn as a temporary schoolhouse. A floor was laid in the south side of their new barn, along with the addition of a small wood-burning heater, and classes began. The Schermans homesteaded in Anza in 1910. (Courtesy of the Hamilton Museum Collection.)

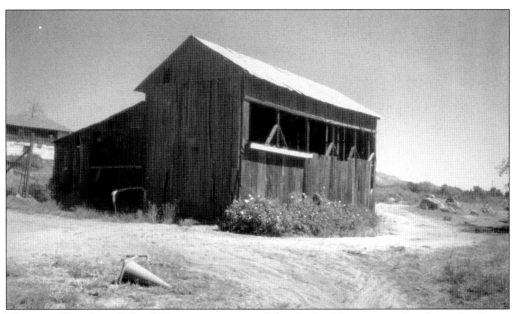

The new Hamilton School District was named for the highly respected early settler James Hamilton, who had died 16 years previously. To build the Hamilton School, the men in the valley hauled the needed lumber up the mountain from San Jacinto over the dirt roads in horse-drawn wagons. Until the new school was completed in September 1914, classes continued to be held in the Scherman barn (above). The new Hamilton School (below), now sometimes called the "little red schoolhouse," was never red until recent years. It was more often white, tan, pale green, or whatever color paint was available. (Courtesy of Mary Clark Garbani.)

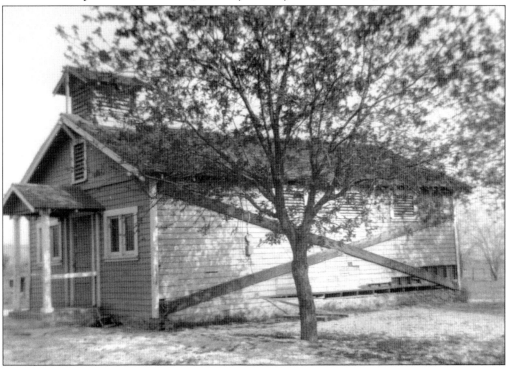

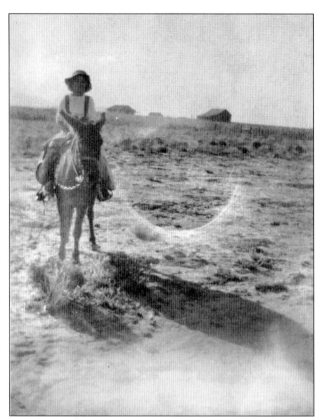

Students made their way to school in any way possible: seldom by automobile, sometimes by horse and buggy, but more often they arrived walking or riding a horse or burro, tying their steed out to eat grass while they attended class. Like many of the hill children in 1917, Rose Cary rode to school on her burro named Brownie. (Courtesy of Dick Cary.)

Clarence Contreras was dressed in his white sailor suit to go visiting. To entertain himself while waiting, he played with a sooty tea kettle that had recently done duty over a campfire. When his mother, Daisy Arnaiz Contreras, came out dressed to leave, she quickly got out the washtub and the scrub board. Clarence proceeded to wash his sailor suit until it was once more a dazzling white. (Courtesy of the Hamilton Museum Collection.)

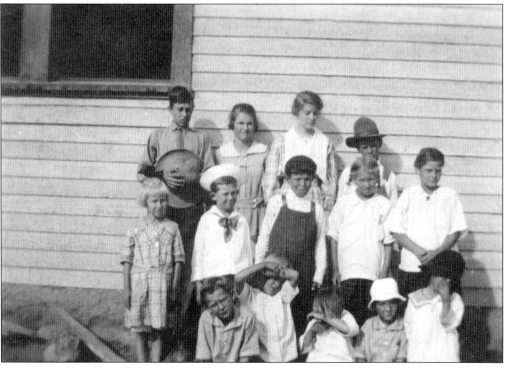

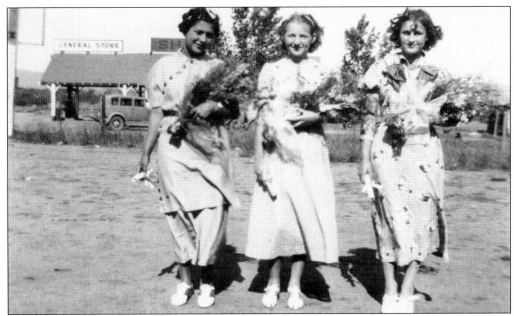

With the typical Hamilton School enrollment being only 20 to 30 students in grades one through eight, there were usually fewer than 5 to graduate in any one year. In 1937, the graduating class at Hamilton (above) consisted of, from left to right, Eleanor Arnaiz, Patsy Rhea, and Violet Stonebreaker. The five graduates in 1938 were Abie Arnaiz, Carl Arnaiz, Charles "Bud" Rider, Pete Stonebreaker, and Margaret Wellman. Below (from left to right) are the 1940 Hamilton School graduates Jean Rider, Irene Tripp, and Clarena Wellman. In winter, the muddy dirt roads made it difficult to get back up the hill, even on weekends. There were no buses from Anza to Hemet, so further education usually meant a stay in Hemet with most students working for their room and board by doing housework or farm chores while they completed high school. (Courtesy of Clarena Dennis.)

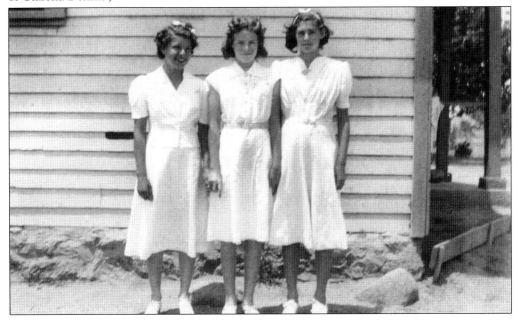

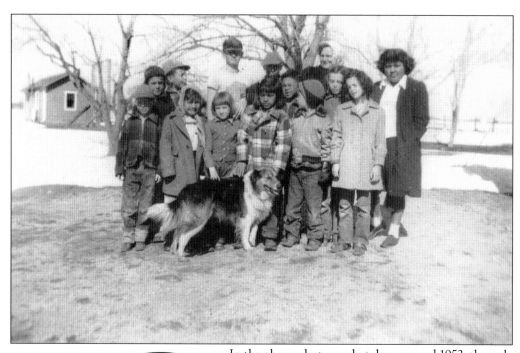

In the above photograph, taken around 1952, the only child identified is Mary Lou McClain, with her hand on the dog. This class was one of the last classes to be held in the old Hamilton School building that had been constructed in 1914. The school still stands at the corner of State Highway 371 and Contreras Road in Minor Park and continues to be used for meetings. In the 1950s, Hamilton School District became a part of the Hemet Unified School District, and new school buildings were constructed on Mitchell Road at the corner of Bohlen Road. The current Hamilton Elementary School is located on land that had been donated to the Hemet Unified School District by the heirs of Grace Bohlen, seen at left. (Above, courtesy of Barbara Bradford; left, courtesy of the Hamilton Museum Collection.)

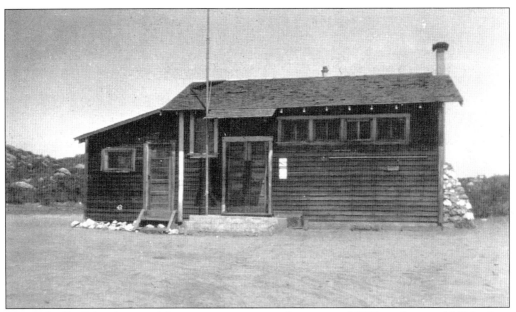

The Cahuilla School, west of Anza, was in existence from around 1920 until around 1926, when there were no longer enough students to support it. Cahuilla School was located across the road from the Bergman Museum, the building with the dinosaur on the roof on state Highway 371 between Aguanga and Lake Riverside. The school served students from the surrounding area, including Parks Valley. (Courtesy of Barbara Bradford.)

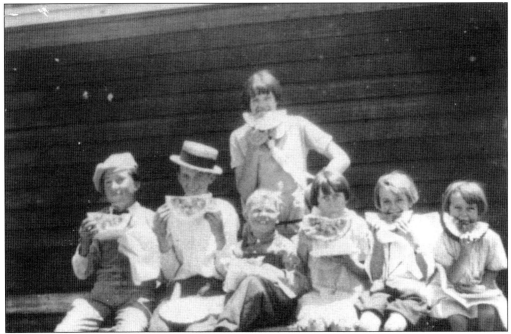

Around 1925, students at the Cahuilla School pose outside the building eating watermelon. Standing in the back is Colette Sharts, while those sitting are, from left to right, Dan Rinden, Gaylord Parks, Delbert Bradford, Edith Bradford, Willa Bradford, and possibly another Bradford. (Courtesy of Barbara Bradford.)

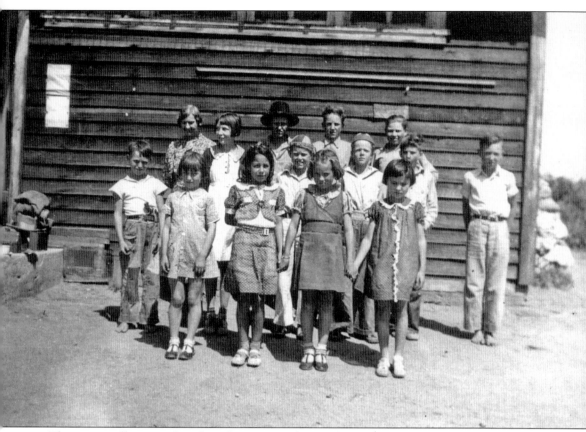

There were still no paved roads in the 1930s, and it was difficult for many children to get to school in bad weather if it was very far away. After being closed for several years, there were enough students in the area of the old Cahuilla School that it was reopened in 1935 as the Cahuilla Emergency School. Children from the Bergman, Bradford, Parks, and Reed families were among those to attend either the Cahuilla School or the Cahuilla Emergency School. The little girl in the right foreground is Harriet Bergman. Usually once a year in the 1900s, several rural schools would get together to compete at what was called a track meet or play day. Sports competitions and games were played with ribbons as prizes. Sometimes a picnic, and maybe a special treat of homemade ice cream, followed the games. (Courtesy of Harriet Bergman Costo.)

Seven

ENTERTAINMENT

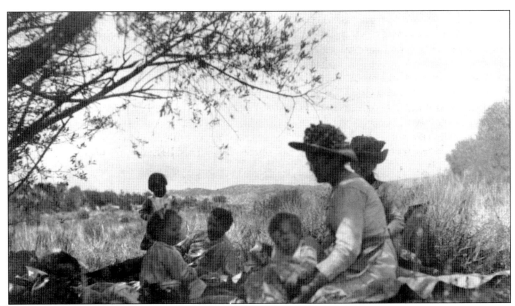

Since the hill and mountain people had to depend upon themselves for entertainment, lunch was often a picnic beneath a shady tree in a nearby cow pasture. Here, around 1912, the Isaac Parks family takes advantage of a shady spot in their pasture. Enjoying the picnic that day from left to right are Beth Pinkerton; Pauline, Isaac, Gaylord, and Inez Tollan Parks; and Sarah Ann Tollan. (Courtesy of Mary E. Parks.)

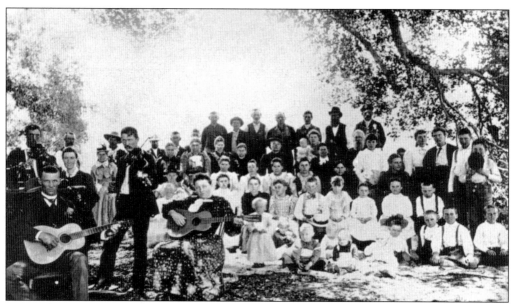

This day probably started out as just a picnic but, as was usual at an old-time hill get together, the musical instruments were tuned up and everyone settled back to enjoy some toe-tapping music. Musicians identified are Isaac Parks with his violin and Lincoln Parks and his wife, Lulu Parks, playing the guitars. The child to the right of Lulu is Lester Reed, author of several hill-country books. (Courtesy of Verna Parks McFarlin.)

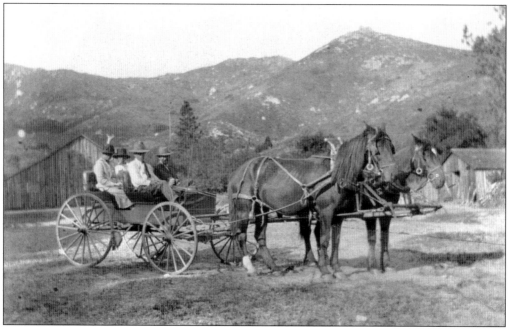

In the early 1900s, a horse and buggy was the usual way to get around in the hills to visit friends. This group has arrived by way of the old road up Morris Canyon to pay Bruce Morris a visit at Tripp Meadows. Tripp Meadows gets its name from when the older Tripp boys from Tripp Flats went there in the summer to grow garden produce. (Courtesy of the Hamilton Museum Collection.)

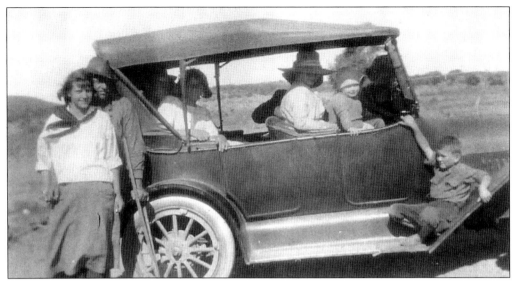

Out for a pleasure drive are Dan and Mable Hall, standing at the back of the car, with Gertrude Smith sitting in the back seat; the others are unidentified. In the early 1900s, Dan Hall homesteaded in the area where the Baptist church stands today. Gertrude, who married Henry Arnaiz, and Mable were daughters of the Thereon Smiths, who lived on Mitchell Road between Bahrman and Bautista Roads. (Courtesy of Roger and Alice Hall.)

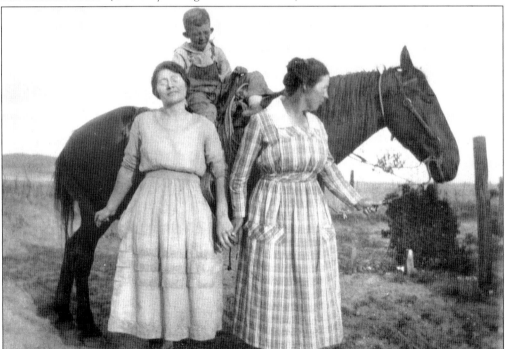

In the 1920s, homes were usually several miles apart. Horses were a normal part of life for homestead people and were used for transportation, work, and entertainment. Any excuse was used to make a visit to a neighbor. Here Daisy Arnaiz Contreras (left), Grace Bohlen, and young Clarence Contreras (on the horse) take a break from chores while enjoying a neighborly visit. (Courtesy of the Hamilton Museum Collection.)

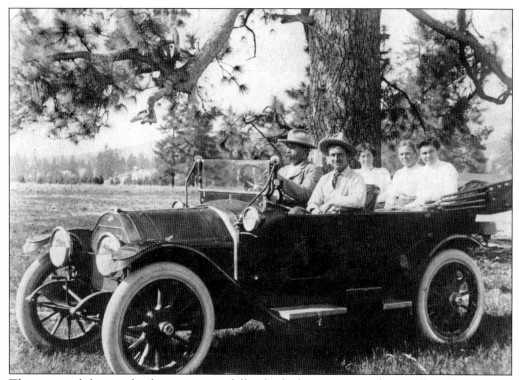

This automobile was the first to successfully climb the steep Hamilton Hill grade between Kenworthy and Cahuilla. The picture was taken in the early 1900s with Manuel Arnaiz driving the automobile. The others include John Contreras (front passenger seat) and Manuel's daughters, Fanny (back, left), John's wife, and Clara (back, right), Joe Hamilton's wife. The lady in the middle is unidentified. (Courtesy of Bud and Bobbie Wellman.)

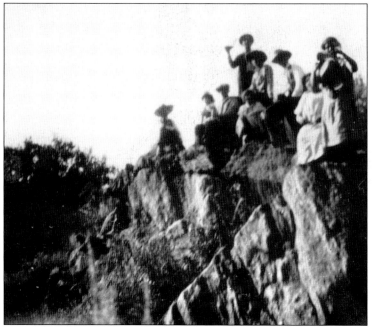

The pioneers worked hard but took the time to have fun any way they could. Rocks were plentiful, providing fascination for many adults who enjoyed climbing them or hiking in the mountains. (Courtesy of the Hamilton Museum Collection.)

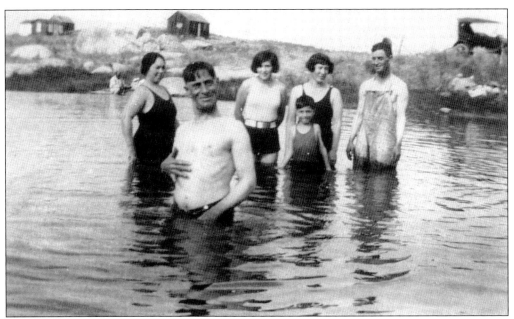

Many of the early valley residents were privileged to be able to enjoy the hot springs at the Cahuilla Indian Reservation. The unwritten rule was that if any of the Cahuilla people were using the pool for any reason, visitors waited until it was vacant. Here, around 1920, Antone Contreras and his family and friends enjoy the soothing hot springs at Cahuilla. (Courtesy of the Hamilton Museum Collection.)

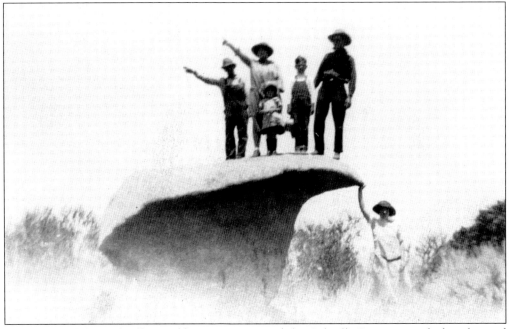

Along the old dirt Cahuilla Road between Anza and the Cahuilla Reservation, before the road was straightened and paved in the mid-1950s, there was a boulder known as Lily Rock. It was a favorite site for taking pictures, especially when going to and from the swimming hole at the reservation. (Courtesy of the Hamilton Museum Collection.)

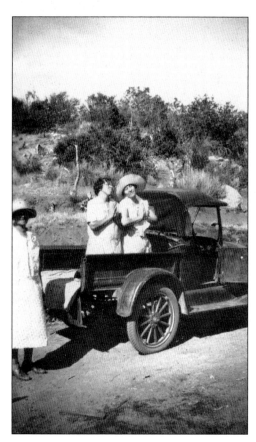

People worked hard and were often faced with unpleasant situations, such as unexpected automobile trouble. Even so, they knew how to have fun whenever and wherever possible. Taking advantage of an unexpected stop along the road for a little merriment in 1926 are Dolores Arnaiz, Marie Bohlen Hamilton, and Fanny Arnaiz Contreras. (Courtesy of the Hamilton Museum Collection.)

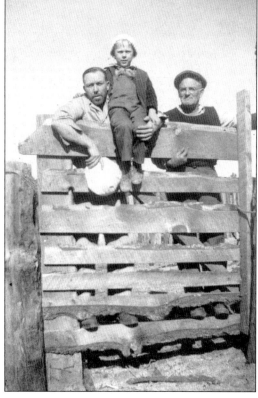

Hill residents enjoy visiting sites of past activity. In the 1940s, the headquarters of the Wellman 101 Ranch was at Pinyon Flats. Years later, Harry Quinn (as a small boy) sat on the old Wellman corral fence at Asbestos Mountain between his father, Russell Quinn, and his grandfather, Harry Caldwell, wondering what activities had taken place there in former times. (Courtesy of Harry Quinn.)

This group seems to be in a festive mood. Might it be some sort of celebration connected to water, like a new well or a good water storage tank? An adequate supply of water was reason for merriment. No doubt there would be a picnic while they were all together. The lady on the left is Kenworthy pioneer, Dolores Arnaiz, while the others are unidentified. (Courtesy of the Hamilton Museum Collection.)

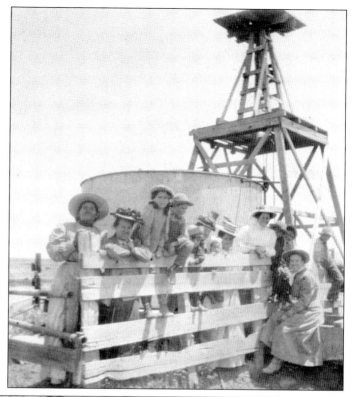

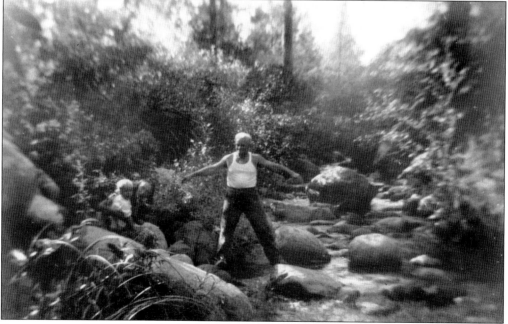

For many years, the campground at Hurkey Creek was a favorite spot for fishing, summer vacationing, and playing in the water. Here, in 1941, Harry Caldwell is seen enjoying the year-round mountain stream. Toddler grandson Harry Quinn and a daughter of family friend, Geraldine Peckstein, are to the left watching. (Courtesy of Harry Quinn.)

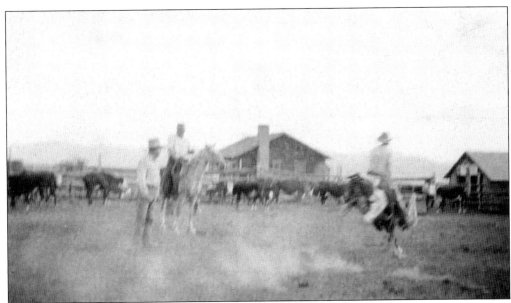

This impromptu rodeo took place in the 1930s at the Wellman Ranch, currently Minor Field, where gymkhanas, competitive games on horseback, are held. When the dusty work of branding was over for the day, there was often a spur-of-the-moment rodeo where cowhands (Jim Wellman at right) demonstrated their skills. Gymkhanas were usually held at the northeast corner of Kirby and Highway 371 with a queen contest and dance afterwards as a fund-raiser. (Courtesy of Bud and Bobbie Wellman.)

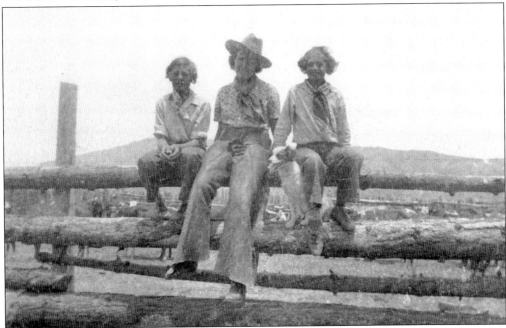

Branding day was one of hard work and entertainment for people throughout the area. Ranchers often helped each other with the difficult labor, while many local visitors and others from out of the hills frequently lined the corral fence enjoying the action. These young ladies are waiting for the action to start. (Courtesy of the Hamilton Museum Collection.)

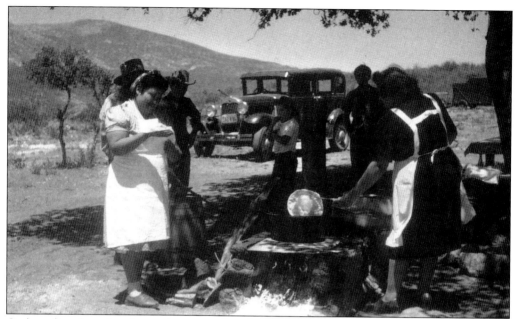

On branding day, after the cattle were gathered and branded, there was customarily time to enjoy food, family, friends, other ranchers, and neighbors at barbeques and picnics. In the 1950s, these ladies (above) at the Santa Rosa Indian Reservation are busy preparing a barbeque feast for the hungry workers and spectators. The cattlemen, including those from the Cahuilla Reservation, the Santa Rosa Reservation, and other mountain areas, worked side by side to make the hard work easier. They usually gathered after the work was completed to enjoy food and each other's company. Santa Rosa cattlemen (below) Calistro Tortes, left, and Frank Alaveras, far right, visit with rancher Jim Wellman during branding at Santa Rosa. Note the branding irons and fire at the far left. (Courtesy of the Hamilton Museum Collection.)

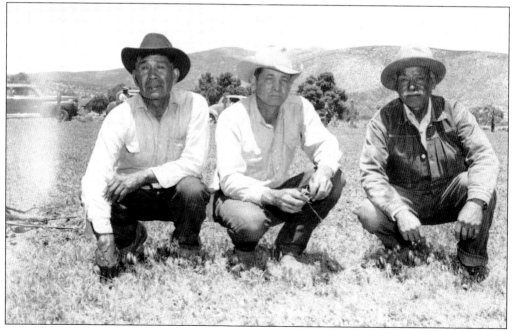

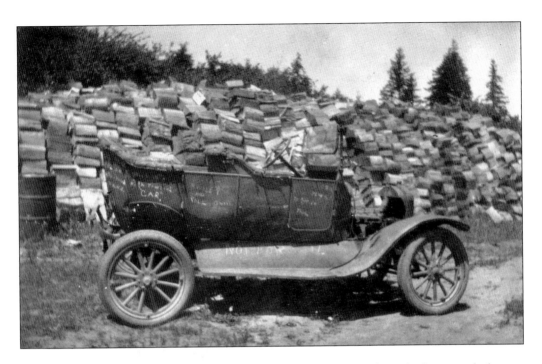

For all teenagers, including those raised in the hills, automobiles have had a special place in their lives since the availability of the first Model T Fords. Bud Clark, of Durazno Valley, was no exception. Clark was often seen as a teenager in the late 1920s driving this Model T Ford (above). In the 1940s, a hot rod was that special automobile for George Tortes of the Santa Rosa Indian Reservation. He proudly drove his prized vehicle over to Anza where Domingo Costo (below), a resident of the Cahuilla Indian Reservation, poses for this picture beside the teenager's most cherished possession. As children, both Bud Clark and George Tortes attended Hamilton School; Tortes also attended the Kenworthy Indian Emergency School. (Above, courtesy of Mary Clark Garbani; below, courtesy of Robert Tyler.)

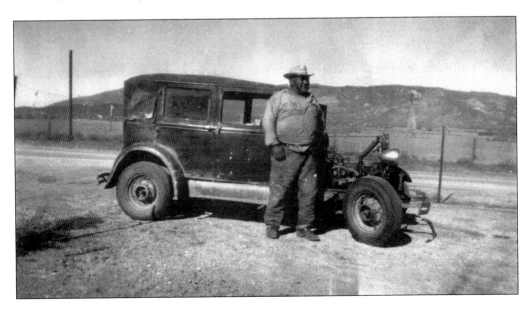

With no theaters, skating rinks, or other entertainment in the valley, young people found various ways to have fun. Many times entertainment included animals. In 1937, teenager Margaret Wellman trained a young heifer named Betsy for riding. The animal was used to herd cattle and make the 3-mile trip to the post office with or without a saddle, but not to ride to school. (Courtesy of Clarena Dennis.)

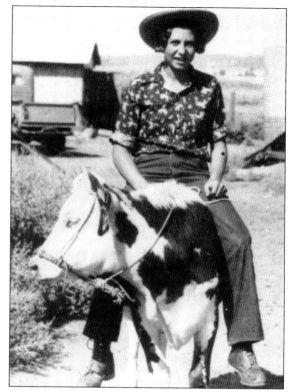

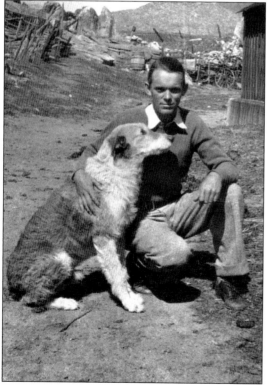

The goal of some teenagers raised in the hills was to get away from the area as much possible to find outside entertainment. Others seemed content with ranch life and made their own entertainment, even if it was just a few minutes to relax. Gaylord, son of Isaac Parks, and his dog Doc share a quiet minute at the ranch around 1930. (Courtesy of Mary E. Parks.)

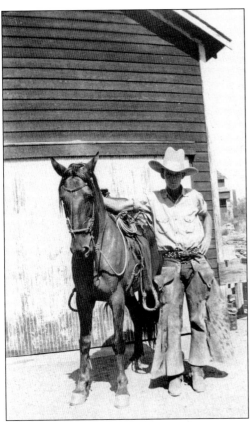

On his birthday in 1928, 16-year-old Gaylord Parks, standing near the bunkhouse at the Parks Ranch, shows off his new hat and Maude, his horse. Gaylord was one of the young people raised on a cattle ranch who enjoyed horses and continued the ranching life even after he was grown. (Courtesy of Mary E. Parks.)

In the 1930s, these two young fawns fell in the water flume at Cranston Ranger Station. They were saved from drowning by game warden Ted Jolly, who heard their cries. When the mother did not return, the orphaned fawns were given to James and Elma Wellman to be raised on bottles by their daughters. (Courtesy of the Hamilton Museum Collection.)

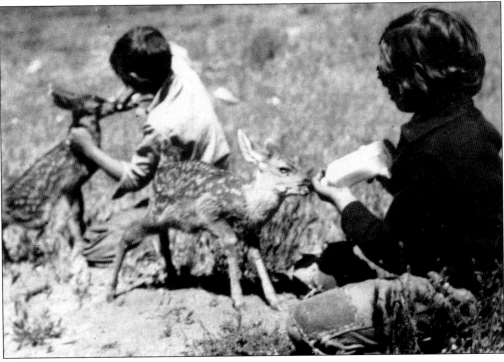

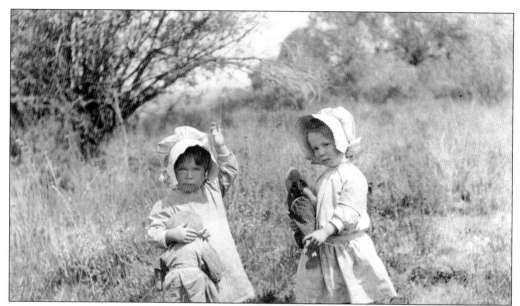

These little pioneer girls in their sunbonnets (above), cousins Beth Pinkston and Pauline Parks, are out on the prairie with their babies. Homestead women, too, quite often wore sunbonnets to protect their faces from the hot sun as they worked in their gardens or did other outdoor chores. Standing in front of the family homestead house are three-year-old Margaret Wellman and neighbor Marcheta Holland (right). In the basket is a doll and Clarena Wellman, a real baby, to play with as the girls pretended to be grown-up mothers. (Above, courtesy of Mary E. Parks; right, courtesy of Clarena Dennis.)

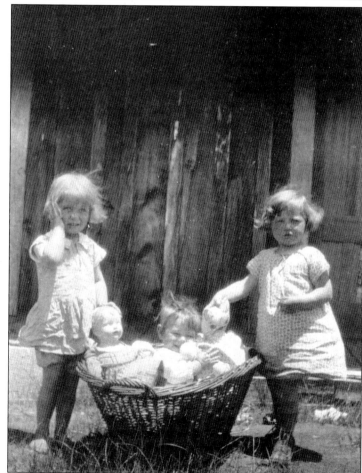

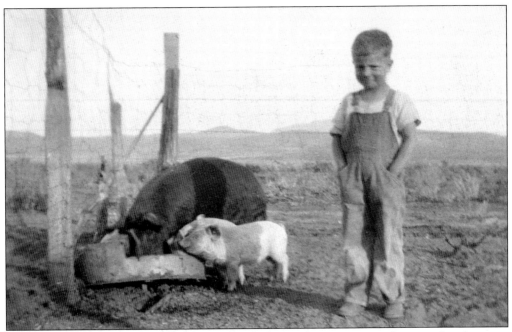

At an early age and as they were able to, young children took part in daily chores. For many, the tasks were fun while allowing them to learn valuable skills. James, the son of early 1900 homesteaders Lottie and Arthur Hutton, seems very pleased with the way his pigs are growing. (Courtesy of the Hamilton Museum Collection.)

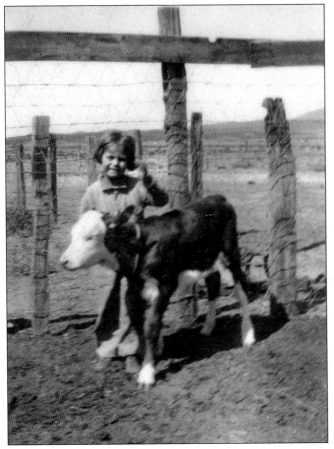

Children found many ways to amuse themselves with animals. Kids often made pets of an animal, especially if it had been orphaned, or a calf if it belonged to the family milk cow. Here Clarena Wellman plays with a young calf in 1928. She is the great-granddaughter of Manuel and Dolores Arnaiz, who had settled in Kenworthy in the 1800s. (Courtesy of Clarena Dennis.)

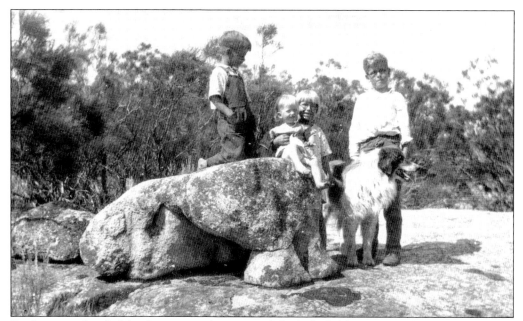

Rocks seemed to hold a fascination for many of the hill children, especially if they could be climbed on. This boulder, called the Elephant Rock and located at the Alice and Noah Cary homestead, was a favorite place for several generations of Cary children and grandchildren to climb and play. Cary descendants continue to live on the homestead. This picture was taken around 1930. (Courtesy Dick Cary.)

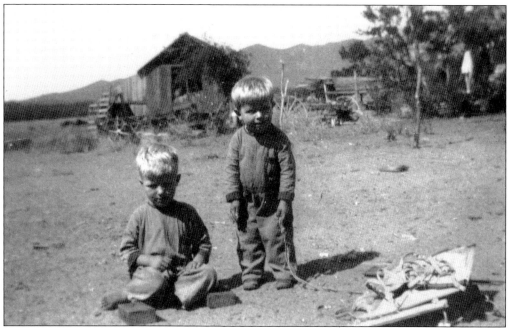

Not having television or all the wonderful toys children have now did not seem to keep pioneer kids from having fun. They were very creative in their play and used whatever was at hand for amusement. Around 1918, sons of Emily Cary and grandsons of Alice and Noah Cary play in the yard at their parents' homestead at the northwest end of Anza valley. (Courtesy Dick Cary.)

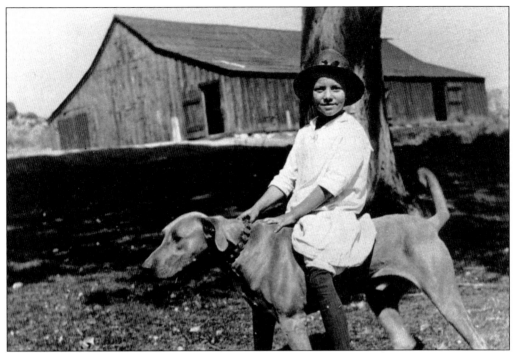

Children growing up on a ranch were eager to try their hand at riding just about anything if a horse was not available; goats, calves, dogs, or anything with four legs were all fair game. Pauline Parks, daughter of Isaac Parks, could not resist riding on her dog Dane. Note Dane's collar that Pauline's father had adorned with shotgun shell bases. (Courtesy of Mary E. Parks.)

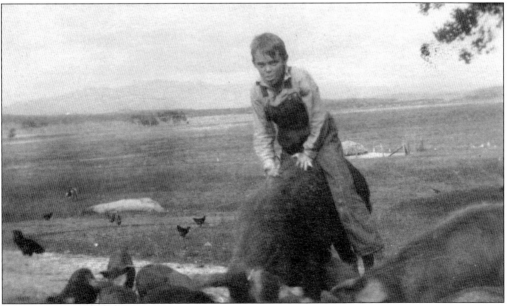

In 1918, six-year-old Gaylord Parks gamely attempted to ride a pig as though it were a horse. It was just the beginning of Parks's long career with horses. Parks Valley, where his grandparents David and Frances Parks homesteaded, can be seen in the background. Parks Valley is now known as Lake Riverside Estates. (Courtesy of Mary E. Parks.)

Three cousins, Pauline Parks, Beth Pinkerton, and Gaylord Parks, found fun and entertainment in various ways around the Parks Ranch. Here, in 1916, they have fun posing on a steer on the ranch where the family raised cattle. Beth grew up to be a successful doctor and was the first female physician at Alcatraz State Prison. (Courtesy of Mary E. Parks.)

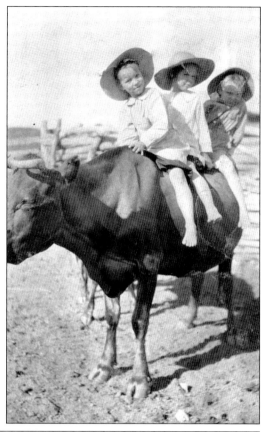

Here five young girls have managed to get an uncomplaining horse to cooperate in their search for entertainment. A gentle animal could be trusted to safely carry children miles from home. The only warning one mother had when she allowed her small youngsters to wander off on a horse was, "Now don't get off the horse. I don't want you to get bit by a rattlesnake!" (Courtesy of the Hamilton Museum Collection.)

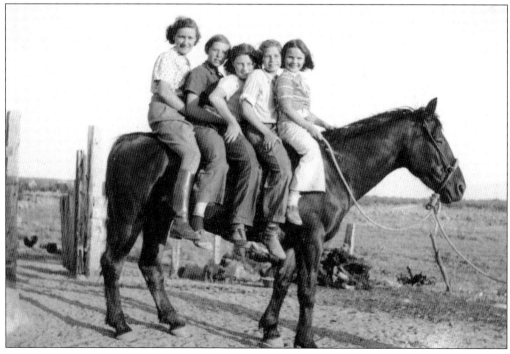

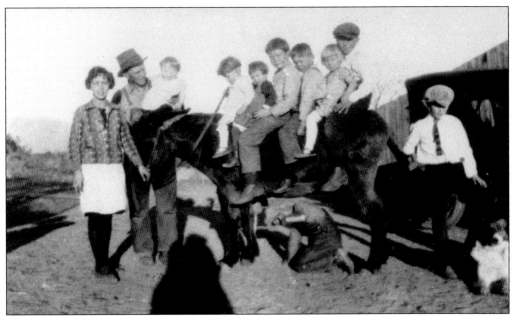

Noah and Alice Cary arrived to the area in 1915 to homestead on the west side of the Anza Valley. Around 1926, daughter Emily and an unidentified man help several of the Cary grandchildren to pose on the burro. The little girl in the man's arms is Alice McBurney, and the little boy in front on the burro is Robert McBurney; the other children are unidentified. (Courtesy of Dick Cary.)

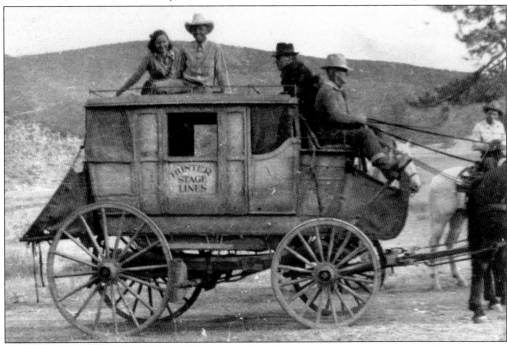

On the stagecoach, pictured to the left, is Edell Durrent with her uncle, Lincoln Bahrman, one of the local men who was working as a movie extra. Edell, granddaughter of Carl and Alma Bahrman of Terwilliger, celebrated her 1939 high school graduation by coming from the city to visit her grandparents and watching the filming of the western movie. (Courtesy of Edell Lashley.)

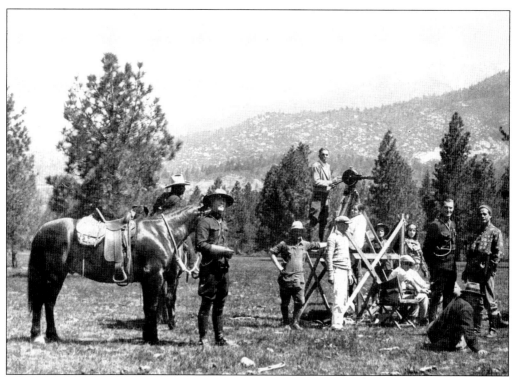

Starting in the 1930s, many movies, including westerns, were produced in Garner Valley, which meant entertainment for spectators. It also meant work for any local man who had a horse and wanted to make a few dollars as a movie extra. In 1936, a motion picture starring Francis X. Bushman Jr. was filmed in Garner Valley in the Hurkey Creek area. (Courtesy of Ray Barmore.)

Many of the men from nearby ranches took advantage of the chance to work while having fun as movie extras. The riders brash enough to take a tumble by falling off a horse on command earned an extra $10. This is another scene from the Francis X. Bushman movie. (Courtesy of Ray Barmore.)

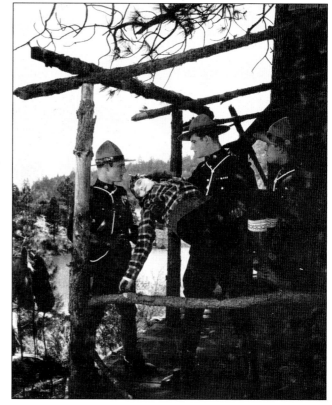

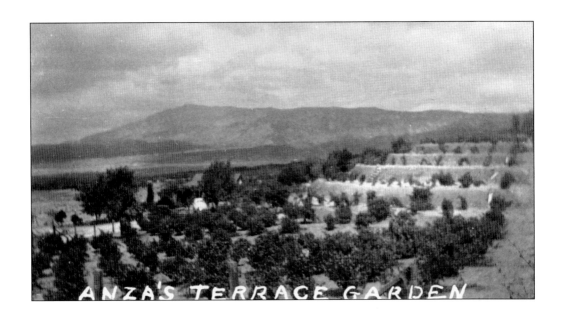

Demetrious Raisis sent this postcard, above, as a Christmas card in the 1940s. His property, known as Anza Terrace Gardens, .was to the east of Anza on the side of Table Mountain. Raisis was well known for the delicious grapes grown in his vineyard, but he was even better known for being a generous host to friends and neighbors. Family reunions, parties, and picnics often took place there. Around 1930, the Anza Terrace Gardens was chosen as the site for the Hamilton, Wellman, and Arnaiz family reunion. Those attending were all descendants of Manuel and Dolores Arnaiz, who settled in Kenworthy in the 1800s. (Courtesy of the Hamilton Museum Collection.)

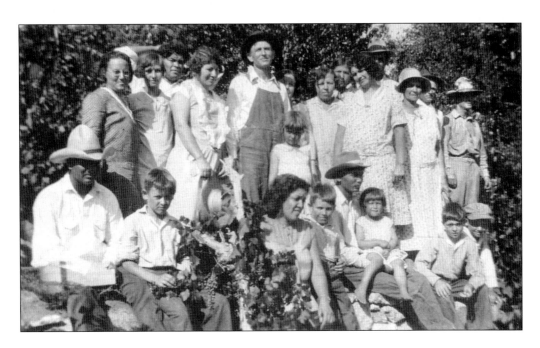

Eight

SERVICE

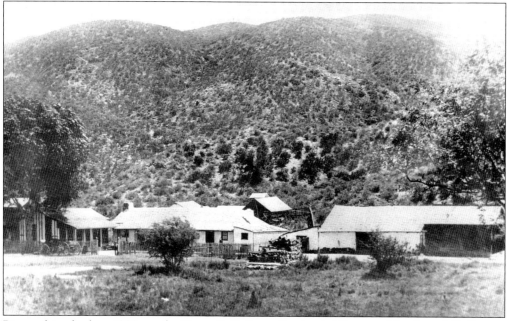

Pictured in the late 1800s at the Butterfield Stage Station is Eli, son of Jacob and Phillipena Bergman, who settled in the Aguanga area in the middle of the 19th century. The stagecoach station was located on the Bergman family ranch, which for a time also housed the post office. Eli was shot and tragically killed while still a young child. (Courtesy of Harriet Bergman Costo.)

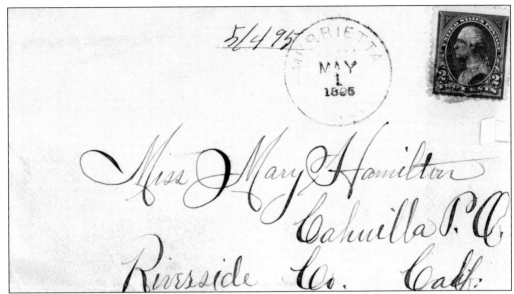

Prior to being named Anza in 1926, the mountain community was known at different times as Cahuilla, Bautista, Hamilton Plains, and Babtista. Many residents of the community wanted the post office name to be Hamilton in memory of James Hamilton, but it was not possible because another town in California was already named Hamilton. Note the 2¢ postage stamp on this envelope addressed to Miss Mary Hamilton. (Courtesy of the Hamilton Museum Collection.)

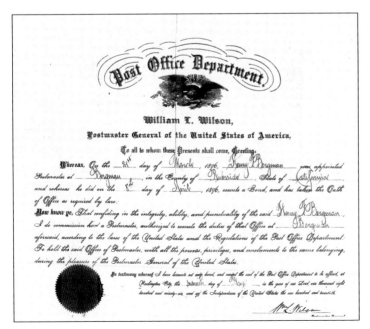

There was no home mail delivery and the post office was located in the home of whoever was the postmaster at the time, resulting in Anza area residents receiving their mail at different locations over the years. In 1896, residents sometimes traveled to Bergman to get their mail when Henry Bergman was postmaster at Bergman (Aguanga) for a time. (Courtesy of the Hamilton Museum Collection.)

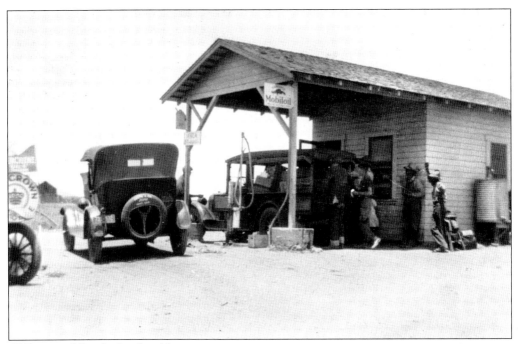

William and Bertha Litchwald came to the valley in the 1920s. They had a farm north of State Highway 371 near the current Catholic church. The Litchwalds built a small store and gas station directly across State Highway 371 from the old Hamilton School building. One corner of the store housed a small post office for a few years. (Courtesy of the Hamilton Museum Collection.)

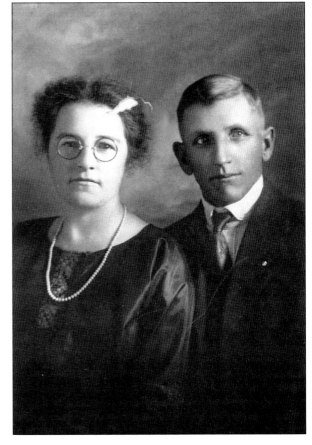

Clark and Nell Devaney also opened a store in the 1920s. When the post office was moved to the Devaney's building in the late 1920s, it became the area's main communication center. People came to pick up mail, get groceries, and to listen to the latest news on the Devaney's radio, one of the first in the area. (Courtesy of the Hamilton Museum Collection.)

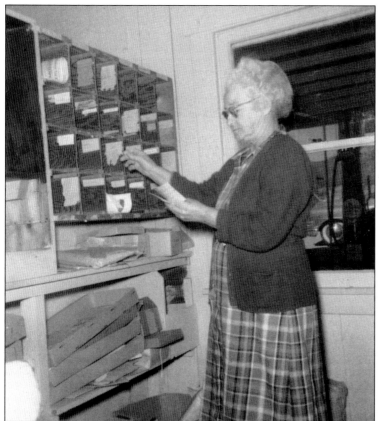

For many years, postmaster Nell Devaney handled all of Anza's mail in this post office, which consisted of just these 24 pigeonholes in one corner of the Devaney store. In the late 1930s, the United States Forest Service installed a crank telephone in the store, making it easier to obtain emergency assistance. (Courtesy of Mary Clark Garbani.)

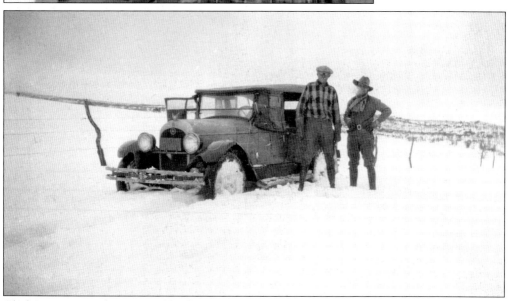

Clark Devaney, mail carrier and husband of Anza postmaster Nell Devaney, is pictured on the left in the 1940s with the mail truck that was commonly called the "mail stage." He delivered mail to the post offices at Anza and Aguanga unless there was snow, which meant the mail waited until the snow melted. (Courtesy of Harriet Bergman Costo.)

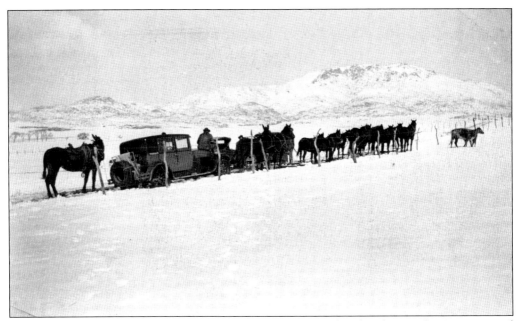

The mail carrier traveled to Hemet to deliver outgoing mail and pick it up for Aguanga and Anza. In 1932, there was so much snow a team of mules was used to pull the mail stage through it as it passed through Parks Valley on its way to Anza. Cahuilla Mountain is in the background. (Courtesy of Harriet Bergman Costo.)

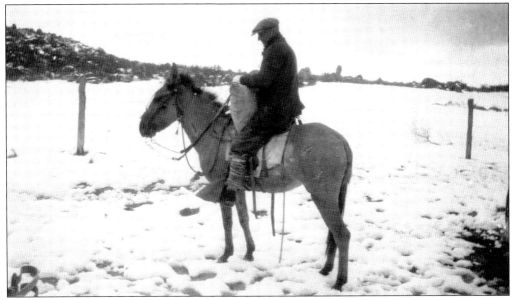

In the early days, mail delivery to the hill country was irregular and depended on the weather and the condition of the roads. In June 1956, due to unusually deep snow, mail carrier Clark Devaney had to resort to riding a mule to deliver the mail, as photographed here in front of the Harry Bergman home in Aguanga. (Courtesy of Harriet Bergman Costo.)

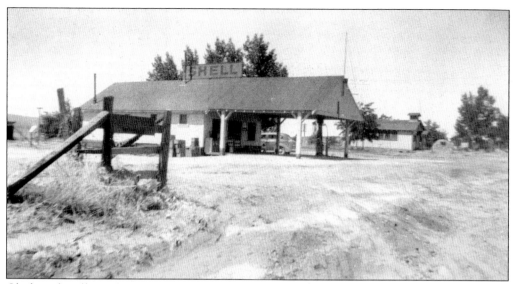

Clark and Nell Devaney retired and moved away in the 1950s. This photograph was taken about that time, just before the building that housed the post office and the Devaney store was demolished. The Devaney store was located at the corner of Contreras Road and State Highway 371, where the bank and grocery store now stand. Note the old schoolhouse in the background. (Courtesy of the Hamilton Museum Collection.)

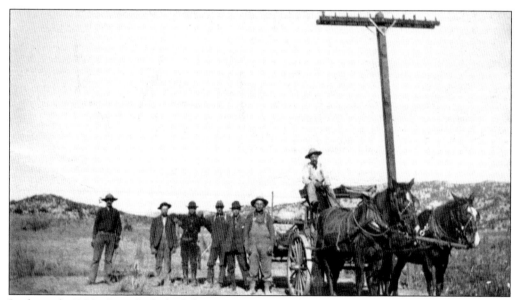

In the early 1900s, Isaac Parks had the contract to stretch telephone lines into the Aguanga area, where telephone service became available long before it was available in the Anza area. Here Parks sits on the wagon with the workmen in his crew standing beside the wagon. (Courtesy of Harriet Bergman Costo.)

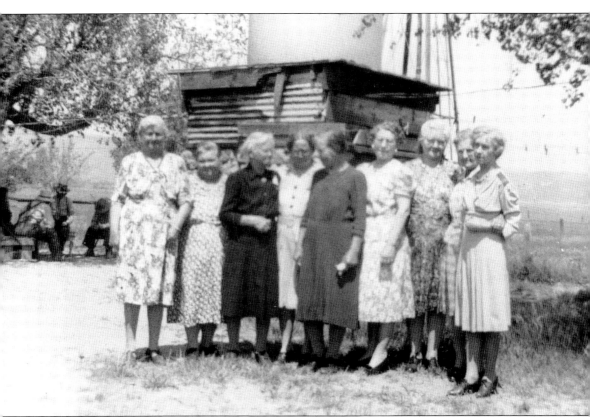

The Anza Thimble Club, established in 1912, is the oldest service club in the area. It was begun by several ladies who used the excuse of doing their mending to get together for a visit. The Hamilton Grammar School and students were soon a favorite among their many projects. A tradition was begun to provide a Christmas tree and a Santa Claus to give each student a small gift at the yearly Christmas program. The Thimble Club also made gift baskets, clothing, and other things for those in need. These dedicated ladies continue to raise money that is generously donated to local organizations, the fire department, and as scholarships for Hamilton High School students. Hundreds of lap robes have been made by the ladies and delivered to veterans' and other hospitals. This picture of the Thimble Club ladies was taken at the Fanny and John Contreras home in the 1940s. Among some of those present were Alma Bahrman, Grace Bohlen, Carla Tripp, and Fanny Contreras, who is fourth from the right. (Courtesy of the Hamilton Museum Collection.)

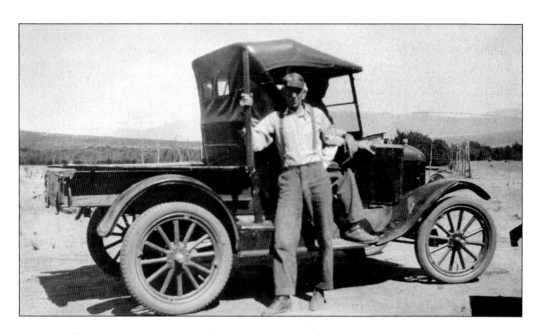

W. L. "Bill" Faust, above, came to the valley in the early 1900s and soon had the reputation of being a master carpenter. Faust built his own cabin, below, in Terwilliger, as well as many homes and other buildings in the mountain area. In one year, 1929, using only hand tools, Faust built more than five homes and businesses. Among those new commercial buildings were the new Devaney and Litchwald stores. Some of the homes constructed that year were for Lincoln Hamilton, Jim and Elma Wellman, and the Art Woods family in Durazno Valley. Several Faust descendants continue to live on the Faust homestead land in Terwilliger Valley. (Courtesy of Shirley Harbeck.)

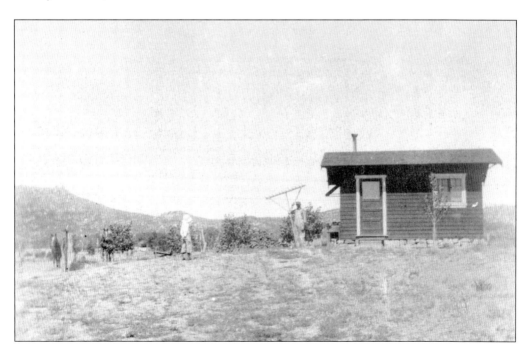

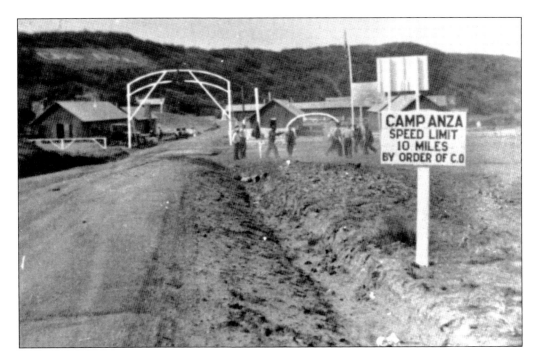

To combat unemployment throughout the United States during the Depression, Pres. Franklin D. Roosevelt established the Civilian Conservation Corp (CCC). In May 1933, the development of a tent city called Camp Anza sprang up almost overnight in Burnt Valley just to the west of Anza Valley. About 200 young men from around the United States lived in tents at Camp Anza while making fire breaks, building fire watchtowers, improving roads, and completing other projects that are still helpful to the mountain residents. The CCC men were soon known for their strong work ethic, making local ranchers eager to hire them on their days off and at the end of their term of service. (Courtesy of Harriet Bergman Costo.)

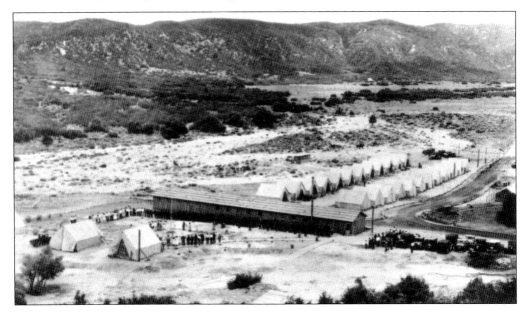

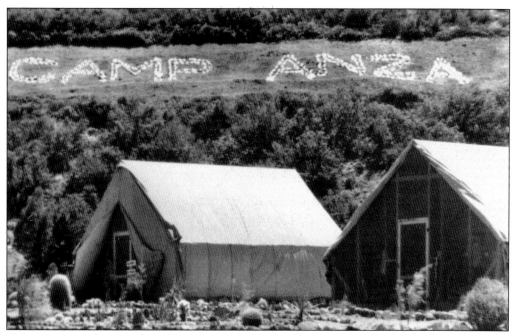

Camp Anza residents took pride in their temporary tent city as can be seen in how they have landscaped their surroundings using native plants and the plentiful rocks. (Courtesy of Harriet Bergman Costo.)

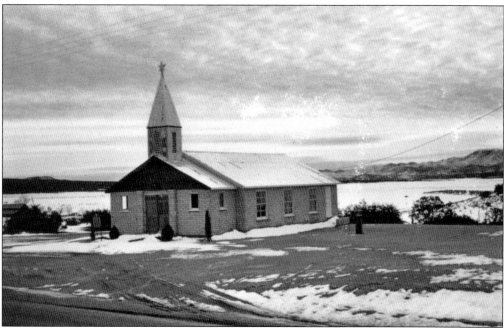

For many years, the only churches in the area were the Catholic church at the Cahuilla Indian and Santa Rosa Reservations. Around 1955, the people in the community built the Church of the Nazarene at the corner of State Highway 371 and Hill Street. Before that, religious services were held in homes or at the schoolhouse, or people traveled down the hill for church. (Courtesy Dick Cary.)

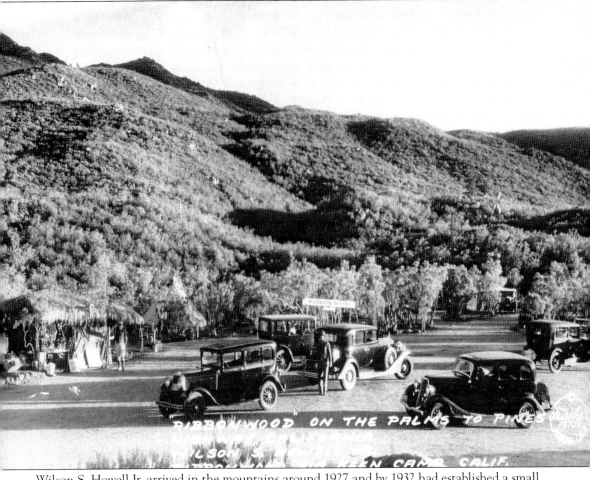

Wilson S. Howell Jr. arrived in the mountains around 1927 and by 1932 had established a small business along the dirt road that later became the Pines to Palms Highway, better known as State Highway 74. Howell's business, called Ribbonwood, was a brush-covered ramada stand located in the foothills of Santa Rosa Mountain between the Santa Rosa Indian Reservation and Pinyon Flats. It was a tourist stop where visitors could buy fresh produce from Howell's garden, a picture postcard, a soda, or a cup of coffee. (Courtesy of Harry Quinn.)

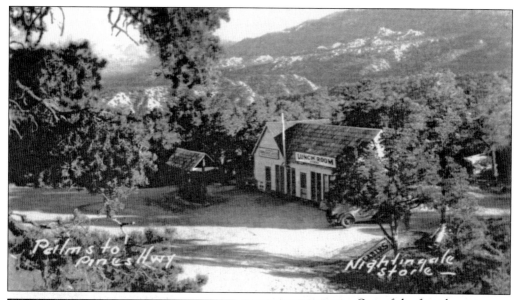

Palms to Pines Hwy

Nightingale store

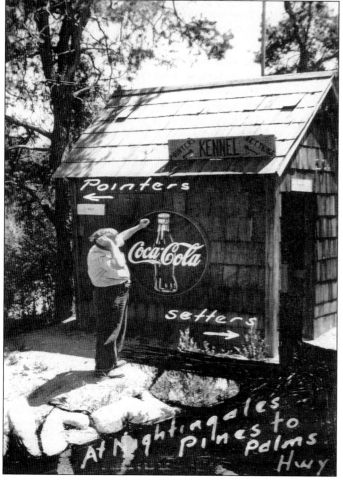

KENNEL

Pointers ←

Coca-Cola

setters →

At Nightingales Pines to Palms Hwy

One of the few places to stop for gas or for food on what was to become State Highway 74 between the mountains and the desert was at Nightingale's store (above) in the Pinyon Flats vicinity near Sugar Loaf Mountain. Art Nightingale's store had already been built before July 4, 1932, when the dirt road to the desert was finally finished. The store soon became quite a tourist attraction. This one-of-a-kind restroom facility (left) at the Nightingale store was an attraction often photographed by tourists. Nightingale's sister Cora and her husband, Harry Bell, ran the business. Paving of the road in the late 1930s brought even more tourists over the Palms to Pines Highway to Nightingale's store and on to the mountain resorts. Nightingale's store is still a popular eating place but is now called Sugar Loaf Café. (Courtesy of Harry Quinn.)

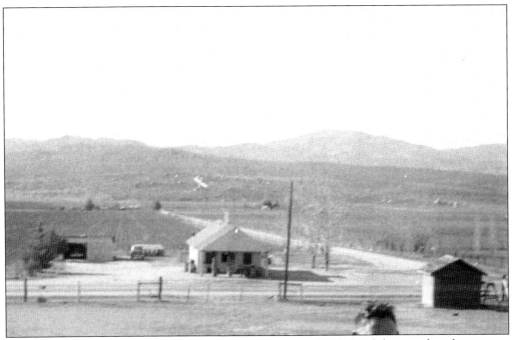

In 1951, Ed McClain, a construction foreman, stood on the hill behind the site where he oversaw the erection of Anza's first fire station. Across the road from the building site is Devaney's store at the corner of the highway and Contreras Road. (Courtesy of Barbara Bradford.)

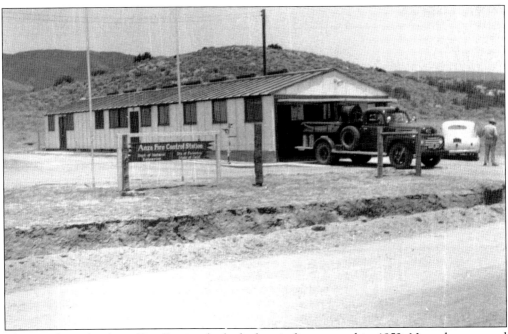

This was how the Anza Fire Station looked when it first opened in 1952. Note the unpaved Cahuilla Road, now paved and called State Highway 371. (Courtesy of Barbara Bradford.)

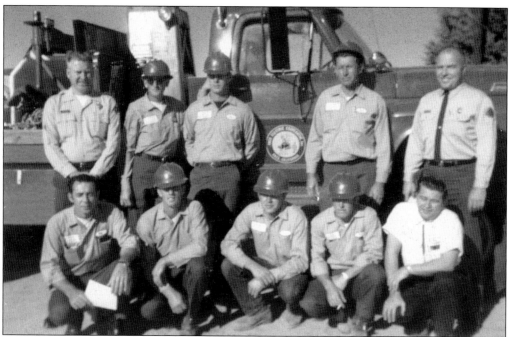

This is a part of the 1955 hardworking Anza Electric Co-Op crew that brought electricity to the hill and mountain communities where people were still living without it or other modern conveniences. The 1950s was also the time that the main road through the valley was paved and telephone service for the general public became available. (Courtesy of Anza Electric Co-Op.)

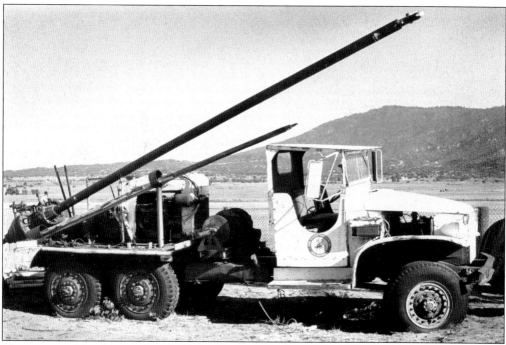

This is one of the first trucks used by the newly formed Anza Electric Co-Op when electricity was introduced into the Anza area. (Courtesy of Anza Electric Co-Op.)

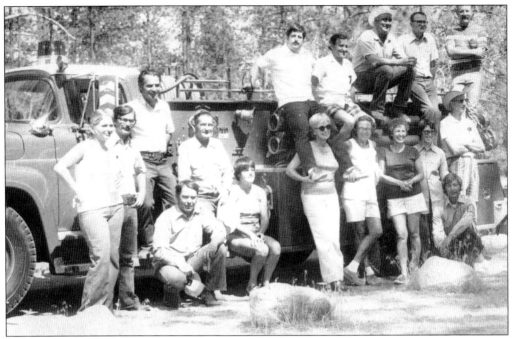

In the 1970s, Jack Garner of the Garner Ranch donated land in Garner Valley to build a fire station at the corner of State Highway 74 and Morris Ranch Road. Station 53 was the first volunteer fire station in that area, although for many years there had been a Forest Service ranger station nearby. These are some of the first volunteer firefighters at Station 53. (Courtesy of Garner Valley Volunteer Firemen.)

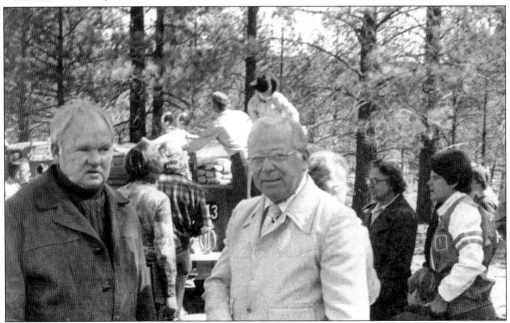

Jack Garner, left, a descendant of Robert Garner and an early cattleman in the area, is pictured at the Garner Valley Fire Station 53 dedication when it first began operation. (Courtesy of Garner Valley Volunteer Firemen.)

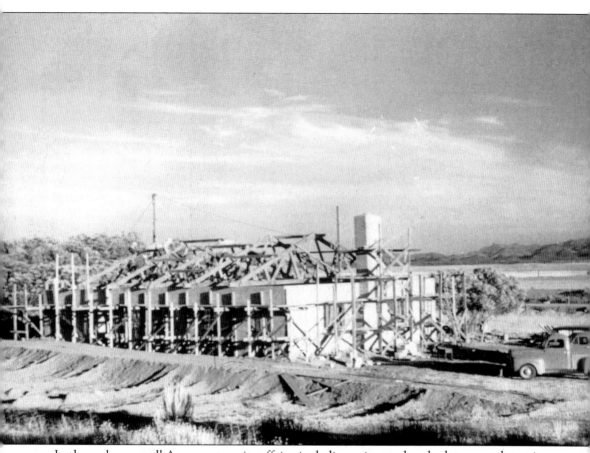

In the early years, all Anza community affairs, including going to church, dances, and meetings, were all held in the old schoolhouse; as the area grew, dances were moved to the Lincoln Hamilton barn. When it was decided that a community hall was needed, there was a great deal of discussion and at times heated debate regarding the building site. Some wanted it in Terwilliger, some wanted it on the east side of the valley, and still others wanted it built on the west side. Some of the Terwilliger group went ahead and built a hall in Terwilliger. It is currently the home of the local VFW chapter. When the Litchwalds offered to donate an acre of land across the road from the Devaney's store, the decision was made to build the hall on that site. The mail was delivered there, and it was a centrally located piece of land. Preparation of the site began in the spring of 1949 with the first cement being poured in April of that year. The hall was finished on June 8, 1952. (Courtesy of the Hamilton Museum Collection.)

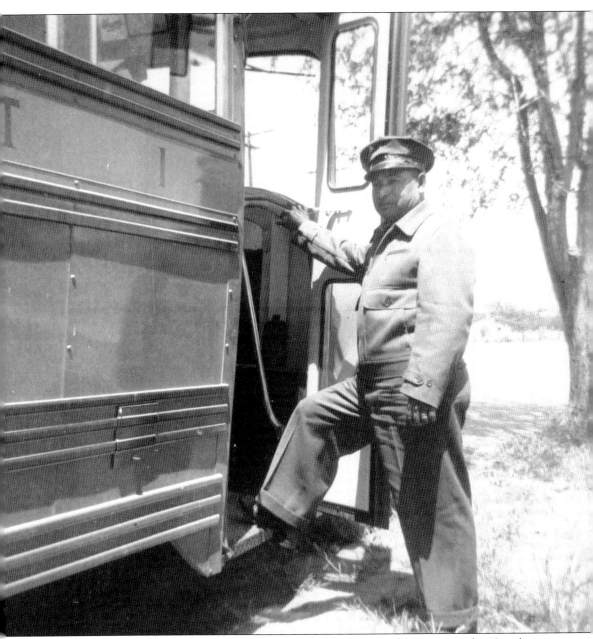

In 1918, a schoolteacher and several students traveled by horse and buggy over the Hamilton grade from Anza to Kenworthy to attend summer school. Also attending the Kenworthy School were six or seven youngsters from the Santa Rosa Indian Reservation in their "school bus," a farm wagon. By 1935, the "bus" from Santa Rosa was a sedan belonging to one of the Santa Rosa residents. Family automobiles continued to transport students to and from Hamilton School and other hill schools if it was too far for walking or riding a burro or a horse. It was not until after Hamilton School District was taken over by Hemet Unified School District in the 1950s that regular yellow school buses were used to transport students in and around the valley. John Pena, pictured here, and Sylvester Costo were among the first Hamilton School bus drivers of regular yellow school buses. (Courtesy Dick Cary.)

ACROSS AMERICA, PEOPLE ARE DISCOVERING SOMETHING WONDERFUL. THEIR HERITAGE.

Arcadia Publishing is the leading local history publisher in the United States. With more than 4,000 titles in print and hundreds of new titles released every year, Arcadia has extensive specialized experience chronicling the history of communities and celebrating America's hidden stories, bringing to life the people, places, and events from the past. To discover the history of other communities across the nation, please visit:

www.arcadiapublishing.com

Customized search tools allow you to find regional history books about the town where you grew up, the cities where your friends and family live, the town where your parents met, or even that retirement spot you've been dreaming about.

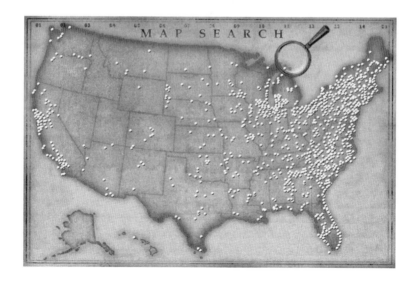